THE VARIETIES OF
DELINQUENT EXPERIENCE

The Varieties of
DELINQUENT EXPERIENCE

BERNARD ROSENBERG

HARRY SILVERSTEIN

Schocken Books
New York

For Gussie, Max, Rebecca, Daniel, Deena, and Sarah

First published by Schocken Books 1983
10 9 8 7 6 5 4 3 2 1 83 84 85 86

Library of Congress Cataloging in Publication Data

Rosenberg, Bernard, 1923–
The varieties of delinquent experience.
Reprint. Originally published: Waltham, Mass.: Blaisdell Pub. Co., 1969. (A Blaisdell book in sociology). With new intro.
Includes bibliographical references.
1. Juvenile delinquency—United States.
I. Silverstein, Harry. II. Title. III. Series: Blaisdell book in sociology.
[HV9104.R63 1983] 364.3′6′0973 82-10576

Manufactured in the United States of America
ISBN 0-8052-0736-8

Contents

Introduction

How much and how little our world has changed since *The Varieties of Delinquent Experience* first appeared. During the sixties this country was awash in affluence—and preoccupied with poverty. Racism, crime, especially youth crime, and poverty itself, were somehow viewed as a single social problem which the Kennedy-Johnson leadership proposed to abolish. The most powerful nation in history could afford to eliminate festering sores on a healthy body politic while serving to alleviate them everywhere else. So a majority of Americans confidently, if quixotically, believed, not so long ago.

Now as we write, the United States is in deep recession or actual depression. Our international allies and our antagonists, as well as the putatively unaligned and underdeveloped countries all around us, suffer from a common malaise. A global economy once thought to be full of promise winds dismally down with the century that begot it. In the United States at this moment over eleven million people are officially unemployed while others, equally idle, are not even included in that category: they have quit looking for work. A still larger, perennially miserable stratum of industrial society constitutes the underclass. Human beings at this level, particularly the delinquent young among them, inspire dread at every other level. Once known as the lumpen proletariat, they were viewed with as much contempt by Karl Marx in his time as by any New Right ideologue of the eighties. These poor, in periods of rising or declining expectations, with expanding or contracting help for them, we have always with us. In the current period of retrenchment and stagflation, as the poor suffer more visibly than most citizens can recall, Washington turns a deaf ear to their plight.

Mood swings in the national psyche are unpredictable. Thus the irony of concern for the impoverished in good times and indifference in bad times. Today in neo-conservative circles, compassion is a dirty word from which even neoliberals recoil. Only yesterday public piety required that something be done for unorganized, powerless, and voiceless masses. That there were such masses, and not just residual pockets of them, came as a shock to those who lived comfortably in an era of unprecedented prosperity.

It even came as a shock to Michael Harrington, whose 1962 book *The Other America* helped touch off Lyndon Johnson's war on poverty. Harrington, a lifelong champion of the underdog, was astonished to find 35 million Americans, something like a quarter of the population, below the poverty line. (Upon further inquiry he raised his estimate.) They included victims of hunger, malnutrition, ramshackle housing—in a word, urban blight and all its concomitants. Within their ranks were the unemployed, the underemployed, the never-to-be-employed and, most curiously, men and women who, though employed, were nevertheless on welfare.

President Johnson, who always idolized his predecessor Franklin Delano Roosevelt, originally entered the political arena as an employee of the Works Progress Administration. This agency was a centerpiece of the New Deal, to whose expansion LBJ devoted himself until military involvement in Southeast Asia overwhelmed him. Guns and butter were not compatible. The delusion that they were plunged us into troubles from which we have yet to disentangle ourselves.

But of the many motives that probably prompted President Johnson's effort to eradicate poverty, none can have mattered more than a passion to complete FDR's unfinished business. For ten years, from 1929 to 1939 and a bit beyond, the Great Depression had been a plague upon the land which more or less traumatized everyone who experienced it. Those bleak years and their hardships were terminated, in President Roosevelt's memorable words, not by Dr. New Deal but by Dr. Win the War. In 1945, with the end of that war, and another one "unthinkable," Americans were briefly determined not to allow a recurrence of anything like the old slump that still haunted them. Accordingly, the Full Employment Bill of 1946 was enacted while the nightmare of mass unemployment remained fresh in their minds. Hence, by the time Lyndon Johnson succeeded John Kennedy as chief executive of the United States, he inherited a long-standing political commitment to the ideal of jobs for every able-bodied worker. Failure to meet that commitment in a context of general poverty, once it was discovered, could only induce a bad conscience among the majority who felt that "they never had it so good." And where conscience was inoperative, fright may well have done the trick.

Fright persists. Indeed, it grows. Year by year politicians make the most of an allegedly increasing crime rate. About the actual rate nothing more is known than when criminology first came into being. Qualitative studies such as ours have yet to leave a mark on the public perception of danger. Even though many of us have learned from these studies that, apart from political terrorism, acts of violence are most likely to occur in intimate settings, it is "crime on the street" that scares city people.

This fear fills so many Americans with anxiety that they clamor ever more stridently for crime control, for stiff penalties and swift retribution. Yet, in one metropolitan area after another, fiscal austerity reduces even elementary crime control. There are fewer official guardians of the peace as private constabularies multiply to protect those whose personal affluence isolates them from the perils of ordinary existence. Meanwhile, in a sluggish economy, locks, elaborate alarms, and more handguns than anybody can count promote growth industries comparable in profitability to the huge media that publicize them.

To be sure, one reads more nowadays about abused wives and battered chidren. The recognition of violence within what is left of an old family structure has so far failed to arouse the criminal justice system, which barely inches toward involvement in it. The street mugger, the burglar, the phantom—not the prison—rapist, the garden variety criminal, produces more and more outrage.

A punitive spirit lies heavily on the people. Capital punishment, a primitive form of vengeance long thought to have been obsolete, has already returned to most States, and leaders curry favor by supporting its extension. A sizeable portion of the electorate can be counted on to vote for candidates who pander to their blood lust.

Similar pressures are at work to abolish the hundred-year-old concept of juvenile delinquency, to equate offenses committed by children with those of adults, and to punish both with severity. New criminal codes which national leaders propose to enact do not discriminate between young and old. Folk wisdom prescribes mandatory sentences for every transgressor. Only inadequate space in overcrowded lockups and lack of funds can keep us from institutionalizing all the malefactors who allegedly have it coming to them.

The idea of rehabilitation is unfashionable. It was not so a decade or two ago. Then the major issue was how best to deal with, even to help and serve, wayward youth. During the fifties such youth were thought to be predominantly organized in gangs on which public and professional apprehension was steadily focused. By 1960 several elegant theories of gang delinquency were formulated and accepted, among them those of Albert K. Cohen. Richard Cloward, Lloyd Ohlin, and Walter B. Miller. These theories were, however, out of phase with a newly perceived reality that minimized the importance of gangs. A comparable conceptual lag had followed the publication of Frederick Thrasher's classic study of over a thousand gangs in Chicago during the 1920s. Collective attention and inattention are as fickle in this sphere as in all others. Gang theory flourishes just as gangs seem to disappear. It is a good bet that sometime soon they will be rediscovered. Meanwhile public consciousness has shifted to other matters.

As the pendulum swings back, criminology can be expected to have its logically unassailable, if empirically unsupported, theory in place. It was largely to test the theory that we set out on our qualitative explorations, leaving statistical analyses to others who were likewise skeptical of a seductive approach that led nowhere. In our small way we refuted that theory. No evidence known to us has since been adduced to substantiate it.

As the Kennedy War on Delinquency gave way to the Johnson War on Poverty, until they came to be nearly indistinguishable, both yielded to the disastrous War on Vietnam, Cambodia, and Laos. By 1973 the senseless embroglio finally ended, and Richard Nixon's machinations distracted a people only too willing to forget all its recent past. Yet the shadow of that past hovers over us every minute of our lives.

Lest the world burst asunder, rich nations, above all this richest of all nations, will again have to help poor nations. And once more they will be tempted to invoke "the culture of poverty" which equates a slum in New York City, or Washington, D.C., or Appalachia (whether in West Virginia or transplanted to Chicago) with the entire Third World. To repeat that error yet another time would be costlier than ever before. By demonstrating the variousness of urban slums sunk as profoundly in poverty as any on earth, we contributed to the correction of that error. And the sameness, we also found, pertains to a universal collapse of values. It is not class-specific as some of us learned in subsequent research among older, more privileged youth. We were far from alone. Formidable works, more ambitious than our own, notably *The Lonely Crowd* and *The Uncommitted*, made much the same point.

Almost a century ago, Emile Durkheim spotted "moral egoism" in the Third Republic of France. A similar condition, whether designated as anomie, narcissism, or psychopathy cuts across all segments of contemporary society. A dimmer view of human nature, for the irremediable part of our makeup, would seem to be in order. By the same token, for that which is remediable, a reconceptualization of the modern conscience is long overdue.

When our work for this book was undertaken in the mid-sixties, we knew that many misconceptions had to be swept away. It was in such a spirit that the present writers and a number of our associates made close contact with certified and uncertified delinquents in three wretched urban enclaves. We stand by our work on both empirical and theoretical grounds. Since policy makers have momentarily taken another direction, it is perforce to the thoughtful reader that we readdress ourselves. May the quest for understanding be resumed with fewer shopworn stereotypes and less anomie.

BERNARD ROSENBERG AND HARRY SILVERSTEIN

1983

Preface

This book is a chip off the old block — or, rather, a chip off three old social blocks. Situated in some of the worst slums of New York City, Chicago, and Washington, D.C., these blocks offer a "cross-cultural" view of poverty in America. To a trained participant or resident observer, the people who live there display a remarkable multiplicity of life styles, folkways, values, and traditions.

A few years ago, the basic idea for this study, bolstered by a whole array of demographic, clinical, sociometric, and anthropological techniques, occurred to the distinguished criminologist, Bernard Lander. He conceived a triple-city project, found support, and carried it through to completion. The authors owe a great deal to him. We undertook the modest task of testing and exploring a few principles that animate his thinking. The "good boy–bad boy" concept, like "the social block," is his, as is the challenge to theories advanced by Robert K. Merton and Oscar Lewis.

Our own analysis is largely limited to responses gathered in intensive interviewing. More and different corroborative data are on hand. We look forward to their publication by Lander and his associates. The study enjoyed multiple sponsorship: that of the Lavanburg Corner House Foundation, the University of Notre Dame, and the Office of Juvenile Delinquency and Youth Crime (later Youth Development), whose backing we are happy to acknowledge.

Our thanks to Ramón Diaz of the East Harlem Protestant Parish, Louise and F. William Howton, Olga Tomei, Norma Solomon, Lois Bernfeld, and Benita Kline for their help in New York; A. J. Franklin, Arthur Pearl, Millicent Davis, Barbara Johnson, and Abe Davis for theirs in Washington; and the Diamonds, Melvyn and Jo Ann, as well as their assistants, in Chicago. As always, our colleague Joseph Bensman, has helped. We owe a special debt to Israel Gerver, formerly of the Office of Juvenile Delinquency and Youth Development and at present sociologist with the Joint Commission on Mental Health of Children, Inc., and Emmanuel Geltman. Regretfully, there are others who must remain anonymous. They and we well know their value.

Finally, our deepest appreciation is reserved for the many cooperative respondents who taught us so much.

B.R.
H.S.

But besides the two obvious advantages of surveying, as it were in a picture, the true beauty of virtue, and deformity of vice, we may moreover learn from Plutarch, Nepos, Suetonius, and other biographers, this useful lesson — not too hastily, nor in the gross, to bestow either our praise or censure; since we shall often find such a mixture of good and evil in the same character, that it may require a very accurate judgment, and a very elaborate inquiry, to determine on which side the balance turns: for though we sometimes meet with an Aristides or a Brutus, a Lysander or a Nero, yet far the greater number are of the mixed kind, neither totally good nor bad; their greatest virtues being obscured and allayed by their vices, and those again softened and coloured over by their virtues.

Henry Fielding, *The History of the Life of the Late Mr. Jonathan Wild The Great*

1 An Introduction to Delinquency

David Matza, a contemporary sociologist, begins his incisive study, *Delinquency and Drift*, by remarking:[1]

> Each of us carries in mind pictures of a variety of social statuses; among these is one of the juvenile delinquent. Our basic conceptions of the juvenile delinquent, and those of other contemporary figures, are imbedded in these pictures. Consequently, research frequently does not progress deeply enough to offend and thus qualify our conceptions. Research typically is guided by basic conceptions rather than being designed to question them.

The research reported in this book, whatever its other failings, *was* designed to offend, challenge, question, and thereby perhaps to modify certain basic conceptions. Whether, along with the ongoing work of many able practitioners, it will also serve to dispel every dubious stereotype of the juvenile delinquent, is more problematic.

That there is such a thing as a delinquent stereotype is offensive to the principles of social scientific inquiry, for the working of sociological theory requires the scrupulous avoidance of oversimplification, overclassification, and overcategorization.

[1] David Matza, *Delinquency and Drift* (New York: John Wiley and Sons, 1964), p. 1.

At least, so it would be. Theory, though logical and orderly, is also subtle and complex. Thus, if our procedures are correct, it should not stereotype. The "common man," we like to believe, may be guilty of simplistic and inaccurate imagery, but not the social scientist.

Unfortunately, the history of delinquency studies suggests more guilt than innocence, whatever our scientific objectives. The hazards of theory building and conceptions about delinquents, as Matza suggests, may well produce that which we endeavor to avoid, especially if it proceeds too long without sufficient empiricism — that is, without stopping and taking a hard observational journey and carefully checking what might be called our scientific, theoretical stereotype. The traditions of delinquency study too frequently have served stereotypic thinking. Only occasionally, when reality collides with implausible conceptions, have we revamped our notions, followed soon after by the same hazardous process. In general, theory has been the rule, empiricism the exception to it.

And each time we think that at last an unshakable picture or a central element of it has been banished from our minds, its vivid afterimage arises to befuddle us once again. For example, even as we write late in 1968, a "new" genetic theory, soberly entertained in scientific circles, is being trumpeted through the mass media to a credulous public. This new theory of crime causation is based upon alleged chromosomal assortment; it purports to explain acts of violence, especially murder. The burden of proof for people who approach a social problem this way, no matter how sophisticated their biochemical knowledge may be, is a very heavy one. Modern genetics dazzles us when the subject is drosophila. Its premature and probably inappropriate application to man in his sea of troubles obscures more than it enlightens.

To students of crime and delinquency, the story has been twice-told, then thrice-told — and no end is in sight. Laid to rest over and over, biological determinism keeps springing back to life. We can only marvel at the power of this phoenix which is regularly resurrected on the ashes of all criminological data so far adduced, inferred, collected, or imagined. Successive incarnations antedate the systematic study of lawbreakers, and in one form or another can be expected to outlast it as well.

No doubt this fixation will remain with us — somewhere off in a corner or, more likely, on splendid display — until the end of time. The labels change; the fixation does not. No decline of interest in organic degeneracy, genotypic and phenotypic physical stigmata, constitutional deformation, defective makeup and native incapacity is to be expected. Some people will go on indefatigably attempting to connect body build and body chemistry with breaches of the law. We cannot simply leave them to their strange devices. An etiological theory, which claims to account for the origins of delinquency, may, and in our day often does, become the springboard for public policy. Whenever a majority of citizens agree that sex deviates are organic degenerates, we are on our way, at best, to a law which will require them to be sterilized. Soon the specter of eugenics, of extirpating lower breeds and fostering higher breeds, looms too large for decent comfort.

Like more and more of their colleagues, the authors of this book take another tack. They believe that what at present goes by the name of juvenile delinquency is universal, and that it has never been otherwise. In every society known to us, a certain number of minors have also been transgressors. And, when troubled by the delinquency in their midst, members of every society have sought to account for that phenomenon. The threat posed by "ungovernable youth" has provoked a multitude of reactions and led to a variety of explanations. So, for example, in Victorian England, Charles Dickens parodied a popular notion when he had his Mr. Bumble exclaim that Oliver Twist's violence was nurtured on meat rather than gruel. (Alter the diet and you "rehabilitate" the child!)[2]

Though nutritional explanations are no longer fashionable, theories of physiological disorder have been persistently influential. From Cesare Lombroso's craniology in the nineteenth century to Ernest Albert Hooton's racist aberrations and William Sheldon's

---

[2]Charles Dickens, *Oliver Twist* (New York: E. P. Dutton, 1907), p. 48.

> "Meat, ma'am, meat," replied Bumble, with stern emphasis. "You've over-fed him, ma'am. You've raised a artificial soul and spirit in him, ma'am, unbecoming a person of his condition: as the board, Mrs. Sowerberry, who are practical philosophers, will tell you. What have paupers to do with soul or spirit? It's quite enough that we let 'em have live bodies. If you had kept the boy on gruel, ma'am, this would never have happened."

somatotypes, constitutional stigmata have been considered the seedbed of criminality.[3] Only of late have widely accepted theories of delinquency reflected psychological and sociological premises. Today one must consider the complex network of small-group, family, and community interaction as a major source of human "deviation." That is to say, respectable criminology is finally shifting from demonology to scientific inquiry.

Few subjects are more thoroughly studied than delinquency, and with good reason. In this sphere, personal alarm competes with economic calculation — to which it may be subordinated in official quarters. Crime presents many objectionable features, not the least of which is that it costs money. No one can accurately measure the financial drain which, however, is certainly considerable. In a culture where the cash nexus has much to do with shaping morals, "experts" feel heavy pressure to find a remedy, cut the loss, declare war on crime, and stamp it out. Moral and financial accounts are to be settled simultaneously.

In part, the moral settlement rests on our conception of the delinquent to which, unfortunately, social science has made a heavy contribution. Consider the stereotype — a delinquent is a hedonistic gang warlord, full of evil (not mischief) and acting out of powerful psychological and social constraints (he could hardly do otherwise) to engage in antisocial and illegal acts.

This is the core about which a cluster of related and highly debatable assumptions are harbored by numerous professionals and nonprofessionals. This point would not be worth laboring; yet it is precisely these assumptions which are crucial to this study, if only because we propose to cast further doubt upon them.

Current fashion favors a criminological school whose champions are more persuasive, more logical, and more objective than most of their predecessors. They have forsworn biological determinism — only to adopt a conscious or unconscious, direct or indirect, partial or total form of economic determinism. Conservative func-

---

[3] Cesare Lombroso, *Criminal Man* (New York: Putnam, 1911); Ernest A. Hooton, *Crime and the Man* (Cambridge: Harvard University Press, 1939); William H. Sheldon, *Varieties of Delinquent Youth: An Introduction to Constitutional Psychiatry* (New York: Harper, 1949).

tionalists and radical Marxists have in common a point of view which is both plausible and insupportable. Common sense, bolstered by crime statistics, points unmistakably to the conclusion that poverty causes delinquency. Edwin E. Sutherland seemed to have dashed that simplistic judgment decades ago by underscoring the importance of white-collar crime, that is, crime committed by reputable people.[4] Not so. He failed. All the same, ours is the richest and, officially, the most criminalistic country on earth. So noticeable is the correlation between economic development and a rising crime rate that many observers now turn the formula on its head: they contend that *affluence* causes crime.

Despite all this, a significant number of us have come to be disenthralled with, and disentangled from, the enticements of economism. Therefore, in what follows, these writers will criticize that point of view on logical and sociological grounds. We must add that those grounds are anything but exclusive to us. He who attends our words will hear only one more voice in a growing chorus of opposition. We are not the first to have underscored gross imperfections in existing theory. Nor did we discover the worthlessness of official crime statistics — whence many of these imperfections derive. Indeed, we are latecomers. The pioneer work of demolition has already been completed — all credit to those who have gone before. They cleared much of the ground. We would argue that a bit of it is still too littered. In the interests of better conceptual sanitation, more work must be done. We offer this modest report as a contribution to that end.

There are two social scientists who have powerfully articulated the case from which we wish to dissent. They are the sociologist, Robert K. Merton, and the anthropologist, Oscar Lewis. Merton, who adds luster to so much that he touches, has been mistaken, we think, in the emphasis which his best known essay has inspired, insofar as that emphasis pertains to our particular interest. Lewis, an astute and devoted chronicler of life-styles among the disinherited Mexican and Puerto Rican poor, cannot and, in all likelihood, would not want to be taken as a reliable guide through the whole labyrinth of juvenile delinquency. Merton's essay and

---

[4]Edwin E. Sutherland, *White Collar Crime* (New York: Dryden Press, 1949).

Lewis's books stand in their own right. They scarcely can sustain the additional weight which too many criminologists have imposed upon them.

Yet, these two versions of economism represent the point of departure and the essential frame of reference for a wide range of studies in crime and delinquency.[5] Because of their considerable influence we will examine their basic premises and their relationship to delinquency: (1) Opportunity and success aspirations, and (2) the culture of poverty.

Let us first consider the article Merton originally wrote almost thirty years ago.[6] Although he has revised and refined it more than once since 1938, the essential differentiation (between culturally defined ends and socially acceptable means) remains intact. So do certain other postulates, among them that: the United States is unique in holding out to *all* classes an identical set of ends, goals, or objectives, mainly those embodied in success-measured-by-money and the good things that money will buy; that most Americans internalize these values, only to discover that access to them is unequal; and, finally, that many of those at the bottom who cannot accumulate wealth by legitimate means, resort to illegitimate, "innovative," unlawful, or criminal means.

At first blush, Merton's logic would seem to throw a flood of light on our inordinately high rates of crime and delinquency. Unfortunately, the light that illuminates also can blind those who want only to see better and farther. Merton's analysis, which has the merit of being testable, was not followed by empirical investigation at first. Instead, it, and we, were regaled with ingenious, but again data-free theoretical elaboration by sociologists such as Richard A. Cloward and Lloyd E. Ohlin. Together, these two criminologists produced a book entitled *Delinquency and Opportunity*[7] (significantly subtitled *A Theory of Delinquent Gangs*) that

---

[5] See, for example, Marshall B. Clinard, ed., *Anomie and Deviant Behavior* (New York: Free Press of Glencoe, 1964). In this work, a sizable inventory of studies generated by Merton's essay is enumerated in the appendix (pp. 243–283).

[6] Robert K. Merton, "Social Structure and Anomie," reprinted in *Social Theory and Social Structure*, rev. ed., (New York: Free Press of Glencoe, 1957) pp. 161–194.

[7] Richard A. Cloward and Lloyd E. Ohlin, *Delinquency and Opportunity: A Theory of Delinquent Gangs* (New York: Free Press of Glencoe, 1961).

greatly impressed the sociological fraternity. Wonderfully enough, its impact also could be felt as far as the White House in Washington, D.C., where in 1961 a new and vigorous President was about to launch his brushfire war on delinquency. Ohlin, with the President's Commission on Youth Crime in Washington, and Cloward, with Mobilization for Youth in New York now had a chance to implement their ideas. We would not presume to say why delinquency did not shrink, in due course, although gangs, or the sensationalism surrounding them, evidently did. The question is enormously complicated. We simply offer our hunch that, among other things, the underlying frame of reference may have been unsuitable and inadequate.

In the ensuing years as politicians and rhetoricians proclaimed with vociferation that they believed in "preserving law and order" — a code term which every substantial citizen understood to mean "containing them niggers" — one heard less and less about the War on Delinquency. Never more than an ineffectual skirmish, that battle was submerged in a bigger, no more glorious, victorious, or long-lived War on Poverty. As in every modern war, the intellectuals had their role to play. This time, perhaps the most prominent of them were Oscar Lewis and Michael Harrington.

While it lasted, and to the degree that Lewis was heeded, the War on Poverty had decisionmakers "operationalize" his central concept — a concept which Harrington uncritically accepted in his important and widely read work, *The Other America.*[8] Lewis's shorthand phrase for that concept is the *culture of poverty*, a focal point for beautifully wrought documents beginning with *Five Families*, and proceeding through *The Children of Sanchez* and *Pedro Martinez* to *La Vida.*[9] To read them is a harrowing, esthetically satisfying, and richly rewarding experience. To use them as guidelines for understanding and eliminating the social consequences of human impoverishment is, we suggest, seriously misleading.

---

[8]Michael Harrington, *The Other America* (New York: Macmillan, 1962).

[9]Oscar Lewis, *Five Families* (New York: Basic Books, 1959); *Children of Sanchez* (New York: Vintage Books, 1961); *Pedro Martinez* (New York: Random House, 1961); *La Vida* (New York: Random House, 1966).

All poor people do live in similar circumstances, peculiar to them as poor people. They also live in circumstances common to them and to others in any single society, nation, region, or civilization. At the same time, they share the circumstances of all mankind. For certain purposes, social science is justified in conceptualizing a culture of poverty, for other purposes a national, regional, or civilizational culture. For yet other purposes, we may fruitfully speak of human culture as a totality. It all depends upon how much insight into a given problem accrues from which level of abstraction.

If we are to advise policymakers on what they should do about juvenile delinquency among low-income groups (so far they show little interest in any other kind), then there are better points of departure than "the culture of poverty." When you stress only what poor people have in common (a great deal) and treat them accordingly, your intervention proves to be more successful here, less so there, a huge success in one case, a dismal failure in others. This mixture is demonstrably present not only on the domestic scene, but wherever programs to assist poor *peoples* have been undertaken. A monolithic view of their plight does little to alleviate the suffering of economically underdeveloped populations at home or abroad. We would hold that it is more useful to take for granted the constancy and the relative equivalence of their economic situation. To do this is to establish a starting point, not a terminus.

Every subculture, like every culture, has a distinctive quality; the entity or the construct or the model exists in itself, *sui generis.* We cannot hope to help the poor anywhere without a solid grasp of this elementary fact. Ideally, germane research ought to precede social action. Coming late, it nevertheless begins to make clear that many poor people, young and old alike, have not been fired with the American Dream, are not consumed with a desire to get rich quick, and do not have that high level of thwarted aspiration and expectation which drives them to desperate illegal acts. Undoubtedly some poor people, quite a lot of individuals, want and expect to make a fortune. Our data indicate that they are unlikely to be the most criminalistic element in their communities, as the Merton theory would suggest. So far as we can make out, at this point in our history, levels of aspiration are more class-typed than society-wide. Other traits specifically ascribed to the American underclass, such as generalized *anomie*, look to us as if they were society-wide. All things economic being equal in the underclass, our findings reveal therein a marked diversity of delinquent (and nondelinquent) patterns.

These paradoxes are a foretaste of the challange set forth as a series of hypotheses in this book. Confronted, as it appeared, with basic conflicts between theory and data, we decided to explore two major questions. In the first, we addressed ourselves to the concept of the culture of poverty and its relevance to delinquency. Are there strategic cultural differences between groups characterized by similar economic circumstances, and, if so, are they determinant for delinquency? To this end, we detail fundamental variations (in some instances, similarities) among three distinct ethnic groups in their values, experiences, and responses to their communities, and major social institutions (Chapters 3 and 4). Then we proceed to describe patterns of delinquency (Chapters 5, 6, and 7). The rationale for studying sexual behavior, fighting, and stealing is relatively simple: they are the major areas that juvenile authorities regard to be within their legal and social purview, particularly as youth are treated at once in terms of both the canons of criminal justice and as wards of the state.

Thereafter, we explore the theory of anomie (Chapters 8 and 9). In a sense, our level of analysis in this area shifts markedly in that we raise the question of whether delinquency (and generally deviance) can be accounted for in terms of the larger social structure in which it is found. We empirically examine the notion of "economic anomie," that is, those disjunctures between the ideology of success (levels of aspiration) and the opportunity structure and its significance for delinquency. We then suggest the notion of "moral anomie," exploring the relationship of moral constraint to delinquency, particularly those *moral discontinuities* as indicated by youthful interpretations of good and bad, right and wrong.

2 Some Problems in the Study of Delinquency

Let us begin by briefly examining a number of ideas (conceptions or preconceptions) ordinarily built into discussions of juvenile delinquency. Most people probably regard delinquency as "abnormal" or "atypical," and conformity as "normal" or "typical." A growing body of evidence, including the qualitative data we have to offer, has so shaken this assumption that its opposite now seems closer to the truth. In a word: most individuals are (or have been) delinquent. (Conversely, most delinquents are essentially conventional individuals.) Only a few statistically deviant adolescents abide by all the necessarily inconsistent rules.

Ours is a study of more than one hundred adolescents. We interviewed each one, irrespective of his or her official label as indicated by police and court records. *More than 95% had committed at least one delinquent act.*[1] However, on the basis

[1] Austin L. Porterfield, *Youth in Trouble* (Fort Worth, Texas: The Leo Potishman Foundation, 1946). In this study, all of the college students interviewed (predominantly middle-class) admitted to violations of criminal law. Other indications of the widespread cross-class distribution of delinquency can be found in the following works: William W. Wattenberg and James Balistrieri, "Automobile Theft: A 'Favored Group' Delinquency," *American Journal of Sociology, LVII*, No. 6 (May 1952); James S. Wallerstein and Clement J. Wyle, "Our Law-Abiding Law-Breakers," *Probation, XXV*, (March–April 1947), pp. 107–112; James F. Short, Jr., "Extent of Unrecorded Juvenile Delinquency, Tentative Conclusions," *Journal of Criminal Law, Criminology and Police Science, XLIX* (November–December 1958), pp. 296–309.

of official statistics in these study areas, fewer than 10% were designated as delinquents. The truly nondelinquent boys and girls, to the extent that we could judge them with the aid of several psychodiagnostic tests, also were among the most seriously disturbed subjects in our sample.

This paradoxical situation, though generally recognized by social scientists, has frequently been ignored in the study of delinquency. The assumption that delinquency is both socially and psychologically "abnormal" almost invariably has been translated into research strategies which focus upon teenagers arrested or adjudicated by the courts, who then are microscopically studied for their psychopathic and sociopathic traits. Influential, and by no means naive, criminologists like Thorsten Sellin cling to the belief that information collected by social control agencies is a rough index of the extent and patterning of delinquency.[2] Those with "records" are assumed to be more or less representative of those who *in fact* are delinquent; by the same evidence, or lack of it, those for whom no records exist are assumed to be representative of nondelinquent or "normal" groups.

To confront this issue in our study, we asked: Do the delinquency patterns as described by the youth and directly perceived in independent observation coincide at all with the patterns derived from official records? Apparently not. First, only a small minority of our population was represented in the official data, although almost all of these youth reported delinquent acts. Moreover, official records bore little resemblance to the patterns which we knew to exist in the community.[3] So, for example, in the Chicago study area where violence (assault) is the predominant unofficial pattern, it is officially ranked lowest among major delinquent offenses. (See Table 1.)

In addition, two closely related assumptions concerning delinquency also required scrutiny. According to the first of these, juvenile delinquency is primarily a lower-class phenomenon. Again, this proposition is generally based on the use of official statistics,

---

[2]Thorsten Sellin and Marvin E. Wolfgang, *The Measurement of Delinquency* (New York: John Wiley and Sons, 1964).

[3]These "unofficial" patterns are described in full in Chapters 3, 4, 5, and 6.

especially the nearly sacrosanct court and arrest records. Only recently, criminologists, lagging somewhat behind more alert journalists and novelists, have begun to take note of middle-class delinquency[4] and its spread through suburbia to the upper reaches of American society.[5] Yet most of the scientific focus continues to attend almost exclusively to the phenomenon of lower-class delinquency.

Along with the notion that delinquency is a lower-class phenomenon is the assumption that lower-class patterns are basically of a single type, regardless of the communal and other social traditions in which they evolve. As we have said, this notion is most eloquently expressed in the work of Oscar Lewis through his concept of the culture of poverty. According to Lewis, that culture is ". . . a way of life, remarkably stable and persistent, passed down from generation to generation along family lines."[6] It includes: ". . . living in crowded quarters, a lack of privacy, gregariousness, a high incidence of alcoholism, frequent resort to violence in the settlement of quarrels, frequent use of violence in the training of children, wife-beating, early initiation into sex. . ."[7]

The implications of this concept for the study of delinquency are far-reaching. Foremost among these is the expectation that youth in poverty will exhibit substantially similar patterns of delinquency irrespective of ethnic and other distinguishing social factors. However, with poverty held constant and ethnicity varied in three urban study communities, we find more difference than sameness.

---

[4]See David Loth, *Crime in the Suburbs* (New York: William Morrow, 1967).

[5]See Edmund W. Vaz. ed., *Middle Class Juvenile Delinquency* (New York: Harper and Row, 1967).

[6]Oscar Lewis, *Children of Sanchez,* (New York: Vintage Books, 1961) xxiv.

[7]Oscar Lewis, *Children of Sanchez,* (New York: Vintage Books, 1961), xxvi. See also, W. B. Miller, "Lower Class Culture as a Generating Milieu of Gang Delinquency," *Journal of Social Issues, XIV* (1958), pp. 5-9. In this work Miller pursues a similar theoretical perspective to that of the "culture of poverty". He schematizes the major or "focal" concerns of lower class culture as "trouble, toughness, smartness, excitement, fate, and autonomy" and offers the proposition that these represent the essential lower class cultural elements determining delinquency. Although Lewis and Miller have different ethnological and behavioral interests, we suggest that their fundamental theoretical assumptions and conclusions are identical.

If we are right, it would appear that positing a global culture of poverty leads to unfortunate distortion and ultimately to misguided social policy.

A brief examination of official delinquency records in the three areas under study provides us with an opportunity to examine the real value of these statistics, especially as they relate to our concern with their usefulness as indicators of actual patterns of behavior within and between specific communities. This is a particularly significant point since it brings into question our capacity to develop explanations about delinquent behavior from these statistics. It should be self-evident that defective data can only provide faulty theory. We therefore ask this question: Do the official statistics bear out "*a* culture of poverty" which correlates with delinquent behavior? The answer appears to be essentially negative.

In Table 1, the offense rankings for each area are listed.

Table 1. Juvenile Offense Rankings for Each Study Area (1964)[8]

Rank	*New York*	*Per Cent*	*Chicago*	*Per Cent*	*Washington, D.C.*	*Per Cent*
I	Special delinquency and youth offenses (farebeat, truancy, etc.)	36.2	Burglary	31.5	Burglary	40.7
II	Burglary	24.8	Special delinquency and youth offenses (farebeat, truancy, etc.)	25.2	Assault	21.1
III	Assault	13.6	Minor offenses	15.3	Destruction of property	13.2
IV	Destruction of property	11.2	Destruction of property	7.2	Minor offenses	9.2
V	Minor offenses	6.0	Assault	7.2	Sex offenses	7.9

[8]Data tabulated from police records available in local or central headquarter files.

Table 2. Juvenile Offense Distribution of Three Study Areas (1964)[9]

	New York		*Chicago*		*Washington, D.C.*	
Offenses	*Number*	*Per Cent*	*Number*	*Per Cent*	*Number*	*Per Cent*
Burglary, larceny, robbery, all types	62	24.8	35	31.3	31	40.7
Assault through murder and kidnapping	34	13.6	8	7.1	16	21.1
Special delinquency and youth offenses (farebeat, truancy, etc.)	90	36.2	28	25.0	4	5.2
Minor offenses (disorderly conduct, traffic, gambling)	15	6.0	17	15.2	7	9.2
Destruction of property	28	11.2	8	7.1	10	13.2
Sex offenses	8	3.2	6	5.4	6	7.9
Narcotics-associated offenses	6	2.4	—	—	—	—
Alcoholic-associated offenses	1	.4	—	—	—	—
Adults against children	1	.4	8	7.1	—	—
Miscellaneous	4	1.6	2	1.8	2	2.6
Total Offenses	249	99.8	112	100.0	76	99.9

In Table 2, the specific offense distribution in the study areas is enumerated.

The only marked *similarity* in relative offense rankings exists between Chicago and Washington, D.C., where burglary is most frequently recorded. Destruction of property in both New York and Washington, D.C. is ranked fourth, although in the Washington study area, assault is also fourth. Put simply, and using official records, each study area, with its diverse ethnic population, generates essentially different patterns (frequencies) of delinquency.

Furthermore, regardless of these differential rank patterns, none of the three cities produces a total rate of offenses for any *specific* delinquency category equivalent to the total rate in *both* other cities. (See Table 2.) At most, a specific offense rate is comparable only in destruction of property in New York and Washington, D.C., (11.2% and 13.2% respectively), and in minor offenses in

[9] See source for Table 1.

New York and Washington, D.C., (6.0% and 9.2% respectively). More important are the contrasting *differences* between rates for assault, minor offenses, destruction of property, special delinquency offenses, and sex and narcotics offenses in any two study areas. So, for example, in New York sex offenses are 3.2% of the total, while in Washington they are 7.9%; special delinquency offenses are 36.2% in New York and 5.2% in Washington. Destruction of property is 13.2% in Washington, 11.2% in New York but 7.1% in Chicago; assault 21.1% in Washington and 7.1% in Chicago.

From these figures, one may infer that the patterns and the extent of delinquency in our three communities are in sharp contrast with one another. The disparities are so great that they justify one broad generalization: any analysis of delinquency as such requires the introduction of comparative cross-cultural data. Without such data we can scarcely begin to understand the nature of adolescent deviation. With such data "the culture of poverty" begins to collapse as a useful analytic or predictive construct. It becomes evident that the information available reflects the development of a highly differentiated delinquency process which can best be understood as an expression of the community context in which it has emerged. Each study area, viewed as a community, generates delinquent patterns which not only are grossly distinctive, but which are also in strong contrast to each other. Only at very few points do significant similarities between these patterns exist.

Of course, it must be reiterated that the reliability of these official records remains questionable. Yet, such data necessitates an extension of the empirical effort, in this instance, to the necessary dimension of a cross-cultural approach as the basic line of inquiry. To treat delinquency patterns and processes as if they were the same everywhere is prima facie inadequate. Furthermore, differences in delinquency patterns in the three study areas may well be an indication of even greater differences elsewhere. Certainly, as our material will show, differences among the three communities are vast, so much so that we might posit several "cultures of poverty."

More to the point, however, is the pronounced variability in patterned delinquency if it is observed independent of relatively unreliable official statistics. When described in detailed interviews, strikingly divergent patterns of deviant behavior appear. We will illustrate this diversity in the material which follows on stealing, fighting, and sexuality.

In short, we believe that the current state of expert opinion concerning juvenile delinquency is a badly skewed version of the actual facts. Conventional criminological premises sorely need serious reconsideration and reexamination. In exploring the nature and genesis of delinquency, we also must affirm the necessity of describing the particular community context in which this behavior evolves.

3 The Study Blocks: Objective and Subjective Versions

Neither juvenile delinquency nor, for that matter, any other form of youth behavior develops and exists in a social vacuum. This elementary social fact would scarcely require special emphasis if it were not so often ignored or forgotten. The circumstances of growing up, becoming a model child or a delinquent are group and community circumstances which demand our complete sociological attention. With this in mind, we believe it essential to consider a few key characteristics of our study blocks and to examine contextually those social patterns which are the focal point of this inquiry.

There are at least two distinct approaches to community studies. One requires the "objective" observer to bear witness to facts and events, but always as an outsider reporting dispassionately at some remove from his subject. Sociological inquiry commonly relies on this approach. With it, one is able to enumerate, to count, somehow to quantify appearances. Such stark empiricism does have its uses. It allows us to describe the presence of poverty, the degree of physical decay, family instability, religious disaffection, and demographic peculiarity in a given area. Arriving empirically at an elliptical catalog of community life, we are able to classify and then theorize about the internal nature of complex social events. Every investigator must first approach a community in this way, and we have, in fact, followed this route.

There is also a "phenomenological" path to understanding any social universe. It requires the observer to gain his perspective of someone else's community life in terms offered by its members. For whatever external appearances are duly noted by observational techniques which provide objectivity and distance, a closer approximation of reality can only come to us through the eyes of those who live it. Drawing on the wisdom of W. I. Thomas who remarked that, "If men define their situations as real, they are real in their consequences,"[1] we inquired into the life-styles of youth through *their* special sociological vision. This outlook is particularly important in studying an institutional network where poverty-stricken youth are regularly confronted with middle-class authority figures, their values and their beliefs. The most formidable misunderstandings arise between people of different social status. Witness the experience of so many local planning and "self-help" programs that have foundered in a conflict between middle-class and lower-class definitions of the world. Underprivileged youth often perceive themselves as misunderstood by those who have crucial responsibility for their socialization. In any description of school, work, welfare, and police, the world as "they," the participants, see it and live it is often articulated in ways incompatible with the perspectives of "objective" observers, teachers, employers, caseworkers, or policemen.

In these diversified social blocks, an additional factor must be taken into account, namely that similar objective conditions shared by our youthful respondents (for example, poverty) are interpreted by them in quite different ways. An event is felt, expressed, and acted upon in highly variable ways by members of different groups and communities. A variety of life-styles persists in populations characterized by poverty, and these are given direct expression by our youthful participants. Whether in social planning, programming, or analyzing delinquency, it is critical that we hear the voice or voices of the community; spelling out the more objective facts, is not enough.

---

[1] W. I. Thomas, *The Unadjusted Girl* (Chicago: University of Chicago Press, 1967), passim.

The Study Areas: An Objective View

Three residential areas were chosen for this study. Each is located in a different city and represents a different ethnic concentration. In Chicago, Illinois, the study area is largely (65%) composed of American-born, Southern white migrants, the majority of whom are spatially mobile. They are capable of fairly frequent movement back and forth from their community in Chicago to their original homes. While they remain in Chicago, internal residential mobility is high. It is not unusual to change apartments within the same general vicinity several times a year. The remaining 35% of the residents are of diverse backgrounds: Negro, Japanese, Mexican, American Indian, and Puerto Rican. In general, these minority groups represent a less transient residential type.

In Washington, D.C., the residents under study are almost entirely American, Southern-born Negroes (99%). In sharp contradistinction to those in the Chicago area, this group is more or less permanently fixed in the community.

In New York City, the population of the study area is predominantly Puerto Rican (65%), although American-born Negroes represent a little more than 25% of the total. About 8% of the study area's inhabitants are white, primarily of Italian and Jewish, East European origin. Although a small segment of the population is highly transient, many residents have lived in the community for five years or more. Some migration back to Puerto Rico occurs, although it is usually only to visit a home town, close kin, and old friends.

In this study, "the social block"[2] is crucial. Somewhat similar to the concept of "neighborhood," which helps in studying the microcosmic community, a social block focuses attention on a small, populous, constricted, lively, and rather mysterious area. It is located in the urban metropolis. Residents of the area interact with one another in innumerable ways. Social blocks in cities often have their own subculture, replete with traditions, legends,

---

[2] This concept was developed by Bernard Lander.

constraints, and beliefs. Members of the wider community speak of "this street" or "that street" when referring to where they were born and reared. They do so in terms exceeding the mere identification of a particular street or avenue.[3]

To a youthful resident, "my street" is much like the rural "my part of town" in which one's sense of identity and development is deeply rooted. The physical boundaries often are quite exact; and, as in bygone days of gang warfare, crossing over into a territory not one's own might be as elementary an act as turning the corner of a city street. The social block, then, is an existential, often physical, demarcation, a place where meaning derives from a sense of belonging, of allegiance to others, and of safety and security in familiar surroundings. Outside this circumscribed area lies a universe of strangers, all potentially hostile and threatening, if not simply irrelevant. For block members, social activities are highly centripetalized. Even if rhythmic movement occurs (to places of employment or farther afield) it is always away from a home base into alien territory.

In all our study blocks, venturing away from them is mostly a collective activity in which groups huddle and move together. For example, during the summer months, one could find an enclave of fifty or more children, with a sprinkling of adults, at a specific place on a beach located several miles away. They would board a bus together, stake out a small area of the beach, spend the day in this enclosure, and return together as a group. Rarely did they leave the limited circle of their associates. In effect, the block had physically, though temporarily, moved while the social community remained intact.

As in many a large, impersonal metropolitan complex, profound localism dominated the social life of most block members. Their frame of reference was invariably the limited locale from which they came. Nostalgia for the old turf could be palpably measured. Overage adolescents or young adults who had moved to another

---

[3]In social science, arbitrary spatial sectors reflected in census tracts are often used to denote urban boundaries. Although they are sometimes relevant to organized groupings, like neighborhoods, more often than not the overlap is coincidental. A social block is a smaller unit than a neighborhood, one which can be more realistically "operationalized" as a manageable unit of study.

part of the city after having spent their formative years on one block, would travel some distance every day to participate in the old round of social life. In this way, "permanent" residents of the past continued to be functional residents of the community though they no longer resided in the area. This element of urban localism has struck many observers as a prominent characteristic of lower-class, ethnically homogeneous city dwellers. Although not necessarily exclusive to them, it does seem to be more developed in their midst than among the middle and upper classes.[4]

Each of the blocks in the three cities has a distinctive outward appearance. From *within*, they are all visibly slums, far gone in physical dilapidation and general disrepair. For example, in both the Washington and Chicago study areas, cursory observation of housing does not suggest the advanced deterioration that actually prevails within each dwelling. In New York City, the overall condition of breakdown is much more apparent, even at a glance.

Other housing differences exist among the three study areas. In New York, all the buildings are four- or five-story dwellings, with fifteen to twenty-five "railroad" apartments in each. The buildings are tightly adjacent to one another, save for one empty lot where a similar dwelling was recently demolished. All entrances face the street, and on a hot summer day residents congregate by the hundreds, some absorbed in playing dominoes on the front stoops and sidewalks, while younger children find diversion in the roadway. During daylight hours, the block is closed to automobile traffic and transformed into a play-street for the children. In the evening hours, the street is open to traffic but only a few cars pass through. In a sense, despite the densely populated surrounding area, the block exists in more or less vicinal isolation. This is not atypical. Other blocks in the surrounding area show almost identical physical characteristics. In the rear of each dwelling there is a rather small and dismal garbage-strewn backyard, with the back apartments facing the rear of the buildings of the streets above and below.

---

[4]The political significance of this urban localism, particularly among previously unpoliticized minority groups, has recently been recognized and well understood. The debate involving community control of public schools in New York City is an example of this process.

In contrast to New York with its teeming tenements, the study area in Washington, D.C., is composed entirely of small four- or six-family housing units. At first glance, the scene is almost suburban: buildings are set back from front lawns and a scattering of trees. But these outward signs of good housing are clearly deceiving. Inside the buildings broken plumbing, fractured walls, and decay tell us that here too we are in slumland.

The geographic area selected for study in Washington is larger than that in either New York or Chicago. Since population density in the area is comparatively low, a more extended area had to be selected. Two intersecting blocks rather than a single face-to-face block were chosen for investigation. Despite this territorial extension in Washington, the boundaries still represented an area in which community identification and interaction paralleled those of the other two communities.

In Chicago, we have a combination of multiple, high-rise dwellings and smaller four- or six-family dwellings. Many of the larger buildings were rented either on a weekly or a monthly basis. In general, the area looks at first as if it is in fairly good condition, although, again as in Washington, homes are badly lacking in middle-class amenities. One unusual aspect of the Chicago block, and a rough indicator of the extreme violence to be found within it, is an enormous collection of broken glass. Broken soda bottles and battered beer cans litter the streets. In this community, glass and metal missiles may be playfully flung through the air at any time. No one knows or cares too much where they fall.

Finally, selection of the study blocks depended upon a fundamental economic factor. Each area could be described, from census tract and pretest observation, as predominantly poverty-stricken. Over 50% of each area included families whose annual income was $3,000 or less. To underscore the degree of poverty, let us just note that approximately one-third of all families living on each block were, at the time, recipients of public assistance.[5] Most of these were families receiving aid to dependent children.

---

[5]Some variation in those receiving public assistance exists among the three study communities. The range of "welfare" recipients (by household) is from 24% in Washington, D.C. to 32% in New York. These differences are accountable by different welfare policies, qualifications, and practices in each locale (1964–1966).

Subjective Views of the Communities

We get another and better vision of the social block through the eyes of its inhabitants. Their point of view, an insider's angle, while jaundiced, encompasses physical-structural elements that are not available to any outsider. They provide the texture and quality that "objective" observers are unable to experience or record. How then do the young see their world?

Like their elders on our New York block, they manifest a profound ambivalence toward their physical and social surroundings. The basic pattern is one of attraction and repulsion. A few flatly reject what another tiny minority totally embraces — the neighborhood and everything that it entails. Mostly, they report divided emotions. Ugliness is balanced by friendliness, violence by "fun," danger by excitement, dirt by action — and so on through a long list of antinomies.

Some claim to look back fondly upon a time when the block was "decent"; almost all feel that there has been steady decline in their short lifetime, and one youngster doggedly holds to the view that it is improving. But, whether seen as bad, better, or worse, it is nearly always subjectively experienced as a mixture of elements. With a little probing, the simplest response becomes equivocal. Thus:

> [Is there anything you like about your street?]
> Nothing.
> [Don't you like the excitement?]
> Yes. Well, the excitement. That's one reason I wouldn't move from it. There are two good houses I could have moved to, one in Staten Island, the other in Long Island. Either place, I'd go crazy in a week. It's too quiet for me.

Respondents spontaneously object to their environment with considerable vehemence — and then draw back from ultimate rejection of it. They complain with all the earthiness at their command of rats (occasionally just "little mouses") and rat bites requiring hospitalization (of one's mother, one's brother, oneself), crumbling walls, dirt ("garbage everywhere, strewn all around the street"), noise, fighting among juveniles and among adults, indifferent landlords and drunken superintendents, constant danger in halls and on roofs, and from cars and trucks whose drivers keep committing vehicular homicide, and above all, from "junkies" — the omnipresent drug addicts.

Whatever their actual physical environment, youth in Washington hold many of the same views that were elicited in New York. They dislike "the rats that get into everything," "the garbage and dirt in the alleys," "the broken-down and poorly repaired housing," "fighting all the time," "too much noise," "the dirt."

Yet, despite many complaints, youth almost invariably evaluate the neighborhood favorably: "It's all right." "I don't have any dislikes about it." "I like the place and the people."

Why does one New York respondent dislike his street? "Because there are too many junkies" is the typical, almost reflexive reply.. Anything else? "Yeah, too many things happen here." Like what? "Like fires and all that. Or people chase each other, and someone goes to jail. Once there was a fight downstairs. No, three fights. First these two men have a fight, right? Then the wife comes and has a fight with the man who's fighting with her husband. And then, well, the woman had a boy who came and beat up the man, and then another guy came and jumped in and started fighting with the boy. After awhile, the cops arrived and then a guy named Mario, he came and stopped the fight. The cops took Mario with a stick. They hit him right on the head. They thought he was fighting. Then he fell on top of a bicycle. He was losing blood." What moral does the respondent draw from this tragicomic incident? The interviewer asked, "Do you think that's a bad thing for kids to see?" "No." "You think it's O.K. for them to see?" "At least it's action, man."

In Washington, despite a heavy emphasis on the poor physical conditions in the community, there is frequent irritation expressed about fighting and noise. One youth, whose grandfather owns a house on the block, sees the neighborhood in constant deterioration, a state which increasingly threatens his investment. He complains about the noise:

> I mean, the little children, because they are . . . I mean for this fact, because they are so destructive, inconsiderate, you know, because they don't realize what they're doing, naturally. But they make noise at times. Let's say at night when probably they

should be in the house or on the porch sitting down because . . . But they're out there, just still playing, running wagons and whatnot, especially in the warm weather. That's when you find them. And leaving trash all through the street, hollering, making noise, obscene language and whatnot.

But his harsh evaluation is almost unique. Others complain about "noisy little hoodlums," and then qualify their judgment with "It's a quiet place most of the time." Or, "Everyone is fighting all the time and these drunks are stabbing each other," and "Those people that fight, it's only once in awhile and that's not everybody because most of the people are nice and quiet and don't do these other things [fighting]."

This amalgam of positive and negative evaluations concerning the block sometimes produces a longing to move away, to go somewhere else, and find Arcadia. Most respondents would like to stay in the neighborhood, some wish they could leave, and others are torn between finding a "quiet, less noisy" neighborhood and leaving behind friends and familiar surroundings. Even the most complacent specify minor evils and weak points in need of improvement. And yet, for a majority of youth the community remains their home, its disabilities nullified by the warmth that the term "home" embraces.

In the Chicago block, attitudes tend to be more unqualifiedly negative, rarely positive. They often focus on weekend street activity when children are not in school and the block is "full of noise from flying bottles and beer cans." In addition, heavy drinking takes place at that time, and fights are not infrequent. Otherwise, it is felt to be pretty quiet, except occasionally when the "guys race their cars down the street."

Young people tend to like their block "even though it is bad." They like the parties, the games, the familiar faces, the friends. At the same time, there are those (and they are statistically insignificant) who like the scene *because* it is "bad." So:

I like it because, you know, around the schools sometimes bad things happen, and I like to do them too, like other boys. You see them fight and you think you're a big shot, and you want to go with them too.

There is a discernible yearning for "the country" — vaguely defined as "away from here," unaccompanied by any desire for return to Puerto Rico or the rural South — expressed by boys and girls who find their milieu exciting, *and* by that rare bird who does not, like this one: "To tell you the truth, I don't like the neighborhood." He would prefer "a place in the country, like a ranch" whose whereabouts he cannot remember although "I used to go there with my brother." The grievance he voices is a peculiar one: "There's nothing to do, really, on the block except play baseball and basketball in the summer." He turns out to be something of an isolate, and more or less characteristically, blames himself for it:

> It's probably not the block. It's probably myself, but sometimes I get lonely. There's no one to talk to. Yeah, but sometimes I have my friends. And sometimes I just sit and do nothing, just stay all day in the street. I think a lot, but I don't know what I think about.

This case is only partly anomalous, for the same boy insists that he knows and gets along with everybody, that he has no enemies, and that he enjoys "having fun with the fellows" who share what they have with him. Even the exceptional isolate (addicts are another matter, for they create their own "community" within the lower depths of a subculture which is itself at the bottom of American society) starts by berating his neighborhood and ends by praising it and berating himself.

A boy, offering the usual catalog of objections (he cannot bear "filthy backyards, everybody yelling, drunks in the halls, fire breaking out under the stairs, robberies, junkies on the street") adds one of his own, "little girls getting raped." With all that graphically detailed, he takes care to add that it is a nice block. What, we are curious to know, is nice about it? "Oh, you have a lot of fun around there with the church and all." The church is the East Harlem Protestant Parish which sponsors trips to Bear Mountain and the beaches and helps to foster "wholesome" fun. This kind of fun — sometimes innocent, often a brief respite — acts as a powerful magnet, drawing those who leave in disgust (for better living) back into the same old vortex. This reaction is similar to that of the late Richard Wright, a novelist-in-exile who temporarily returned to the United States while continuing to curse its racism. Asked why he left Paris for New York, Wright's rejoinder was, "I prefer this hell." (He did not prefer it for long.) The respondent quoted above tells us that he journeys from his new home in the Bronx back to the same old and dangerous stamping ground because in his new neighborhood, "It's so quiet you can hear a pin drop. I'm so used to going to sleep with noise and people screaming and fighting, I guess I don't like quiet. Where I am now they stay out on the stoop, but like at six o'clock they go in the house . . . so I stay downtown. A lot of my girl friends that moved away come back; they stay down more than up in their own houses." Clearly, we have to do with a love–hate affair of some depth and subtlety.

A Discrepant Cultural Element of One Community

In the New York block, one element not present in the other communities pervades the cultural environment. Many youngsters who will freely discuss forbidden behavior — theft, graft, drug addiction, sexual promiscuity, misconduct in school or absence from it — suddenly balk when asked to chat about "spiritism." Their reticence on this topic is not wholly unfathomable: much of it simply indicates that we are touching upon an inexplicable or incommunicable experience. Quite a few respondents, therefore, declare "I don't like to talk about it. It's hard to explain," or the equivalent thereof. That occult or magical practices are considered incomprehensible to the uninitiated should not surprise us. At best, their meaning is extremely hard to articulate. This fact does not, however, account for the widespread reluctance, among believers and nonbelievers, to "talk about it." A clue to why they shy away from the subject is afforded by those who say they fear that others view spiritism as silly, or indeed, that they themselves so view it.

Spiritism, as the word is widely used in East Harlem, may be a synonym for voodoo. It refers to mystical states, reveries variously induced, black and white magic (and thus malevolent and benevolent spirits), techniques for reaching the dead, understanding the past, and predicting the future. Certain older women (once in awhile younger ones) are supposed to be especially endowed with mystical powers. They become *brujas* (or witches), mixing and dispensing herbs, drugs, potions, and other appropriate paraphernalia on conspicuous display in any neighborhood *botánica* (drug store). How profitable this occupation is we do not know, but that it yields an income to quite a lot of "Aunts," "Mothers," and "Grandmothers" is very clear.

They and their adherents act in defiance of the Roman Catholic Church into which the majority of them have been baptized. The practice of sorcery can only be offensive to the Church. It has tried for centuries to uproot such survivals of paganism in Puerto Rico. All the same, it persists — and proves hearty enough to be exportable. The magico-religious mixture reappears in America, where discretion is called for. Hence, when one young man admits that his mother is an *espiritista,* he adds in the same breath, "She is also a Catholic." And those who reject spiritism out-of-hand frequently do so in the name of Catholicism: "Any time I need something, I just pray to God." One hears, too, an echo of the old accommodation Christianity had to make in Europe: "She believes in all the saints. She always prays to them, and if she sees that they give her what she asks for, she lights up a candle for them."

Among others who profess to be repelled by spiritism or to disbelieve in it, there is a common expression of fright, as if attempting to conjure up the spirit world, whether efficacious or not, is inherently objectionable. "I don't know about believing. I was too scared to believe in anything," and this kind of recollection is not incompatible with dismissing the whole business as "a lot of bull." Nor does their fright deter them from characterizing *brujas* as "stupid," "crazy," "loco," and the like (terminology remarkably like that applied to drug addicts, on whose activities it is also unpleasant to dwell, although one does so more willingly). A boy who denies that his Aunt Mimi, a witch, can actually speak to the dead, notwithstanding her nightly visit to the graveyard, is still "scared" at the sight of those things he believes she can do. Thus:

> Yeah man. She smoke a cigar when she dances . . . It bring the spirit . . . I have seen that. She can bring a spirit right now if she wants to . . . When I sleep over her house, my cousins

lend me a knife . . . In the night, when I sleep off, you know, there's a lot of funny pictures on the wall and she makes 'em move. I don't know how. She touches them, and they move . . . They're like, like alive!

But asked, "Do you believe that?" He answers with some bravado, "Nah!" "But it's scary?" "Yeah."

A spokesman for the most luckless family in our sample has an elaborate belief-system which even she unfolds with the greatest hesitation. "I don't know where to begin. You see, when a person dies, it all depends on whether God picked him up in time to rest in peace. Otherwise, he could be around. We believe that every person has their god to guard them that way and also that they have other persons that are put on them on the side." She sees her brothers' difficulties, her own, and those of her family as originating in the ill-will of neighbors armed with supernatural power: "You see, a lot of people on ——— Street, they envy us. I don't know why. [And it *is* rather mystifying — the lot of this family is most unenviable.] And they always wish that we would all get in trouble, things like that . . . They wish the whole family would go down." Wishing them ill, their neighbors bring them grief: "When you think of a person mentally, it hurts more than if you put a voodoo on the person, believe it or not." There are antidotes: "Maybe with that powder, it will weaken the spirit down. Then if the spirit does something, it will not have the same power as before. Then the good spirit will come along and help." Finally, after a lengthy exposition, "I don't like to talk about it really."

A "skeptical" youngster offers his description of a séance. The medium, we learn, "holds your hands — she says a little prayer; and all of a sudden, her hands start getting cold, real cold." On a specific occasion, "I knew it was for me because my face, everything was getting cold. So when the spirit goes toward her, I feel the wind, you know. Then, when it gets into her, she drops her hand. And they start speaking. But sometimes I don't believe in it because when that happened, the window was open and I thought that the air from the window was coming in. That's why I don't hardly believe in it." Nevertheless: "I was real scared. Sometimes they had the candle on the desk, and the water spills and the candle lights, you know, blows away, and I get really scared. I start trembling and everything." By the same token, with identical emphasis, "She got this deck of cards with some funeral boxes on them and two swords across and all that. They play on you, and they tell what's going to happen in the future. But, I don't believe in that either 'cause nobody can know what's going to happen in the future."

The attitudinal similarity by which feelings toward drug addiction come to resemble those towards spiritism is made explicit in this comment:

> Yeah, but I don't believe in that. I go to this church a few blocks away. In there they got all these people and they act like they really believe. So I walked out. I don't want to be hooked on nothing like that.

The fusion of belief (mostly transferred onto elders and onto some age-mates) and skepticism (ambiguously claimed for oneself) is evident throughout: "Like this special *aqua* something they call it. You take a bath with it, and you're supposed to have all the luck in the world. I took a bath with it and nothing happened to me." The punitive, purgative and protective, attractive and repulsive power of various potions, lavings, and powders arouses much speculation. A frequent tendency is to laugh it all off — accompanied by acute anxiety, much discomfort, and the apparently unshakable sense that there may be something to it after all. The boy who asserts that he just laughs his head off at a séance cannot completely conceal his underlying hysteria in the presence of possibly awful powers. And such a boy's mother sometimes believes that magic can prevent him from misbehaving:

> She took me once to a lady who told me about all that happened to me. Then my mother had to pay her. She tells everything what happened to you on everything. Then she give you something to take a bath. You put it on the wall when you're taking a bath . . . If you want to do something wrong, like it stop you. It only works for awhile, three weeks or something . . . Did it work for me? Yeah, but you see, she didn't let me go down on the street either all that time. So . . .

Again, the impalpability of it all is invoked: "There is no proof and no history on it. It comes to a dark end. In other words, it begins nowhere and it ends nowhere. So, that's why people don't even argue over it."

Whether spiritism has a centripetal or centrifugal pull, it is all around: "In other words, people could go into a house, a friend's house, and the meeting is going on, and they just stay there to see it. And they ask to come again." And so it goes.

On the other hand, in consonance with our recurrent theme:

> [Why don't you go to meetings?]
> I get scared.
> [What's so scary about them?]
> Well, I don't like the idea of people talking to spirits and everything like that.

Insofar as these people are positively inclined toward witchcraft, it seems to have the same functions for them as those imputed to the Navajo by Clyde Kluckholn: to relieve psychologically, or to make more intelligible, the material privation of a people who can hardly help but realize that they are bottom dogs in a dynamic society.[6] That society is also overwhelmingly secular, with very little room for other's "superstitious" beliefs. A young person is likely to assimilate some of the traditional faith in magic from his family — only to have it neutralized by other influences. In this way, he is robbed of certain supernatural consolations and made to seek them out, if at all, surreptitiously, and with a divided heart.

Neither the Washington nor the Chicago areas exhibited an aspect of magical and spiritistic activity. In a most critical sense, this fact by itself greatly weakens "the culture of poverty" as a viable concept.

The Method

Data of this nature derive from relatively unstructured, informal interviews with 133 young people (approximately 65% male, 35% female) living on the blocks previously described. In New York,

[6]Clyde Kluckhohn and Dorothea Leighton, *The Navajo* (Cambridge: Harvard University Press, 1946).

52 residents were interviewed; in Chicago, 41; in Washington, D.C., 40 more. The procedure in each case initially involved a complete census of the block by the interview staff; nearly everyone was enumerated by age, sex, ethnicity, and other demographic variables. From this list, a separate roster of all youth between the ages of eleven and twenty was compiled. In the next stage of selection, a list of juveniles with arrest and conviction records was drawn from police and court records. The youth were then classified into three major categories: those without records (nondelinquent), those with arrest records but no convictions (these are designated as non-adjudicated, official delinquents who, in processing by police and law enforcement officials, settle the matter informally with parents or relatives and thereby avoid channelling them into the court system), and finally, those with both arrest and court records (officially adjudicated delinquents). From the three separate but related lists of names, we randomly chose an interview sample of youth, somewhat overselecting those that fell between the male, thirteen-through-seventeen-year-old age group, since delinquency, both official and actual, more often falls within that category. Then, with the assistance of either influential residents of the block or professional resident-observers who were attached to the research group, the youth were brought into our office for interviewing.

The interview itself was technically simple. Two interviewers, in tandem with a respondent, sat in a closed room around a table or desk upon which they had set up a tape recorder. In advance, a number of themes were selected; others developed as we went along. A few of the results, as the authors interpret them, are presented below.

We stressed personal experiences and attitudes relating to acts of delinquency, levels of aspiration, and conceptions of right and wrong. In addition, we dwelt upon family interaction, welfare, police, the block, school, and certain other related and relevant social characteristics.

Questions did not follow any particular sequence. The basic principle of qualitative interviewing is to move with a series of probes from the general to the specific, from the public to the private, and from the least defensive to the more defensive. Further, in the course of exploring one topic, if another one is touched off by a respondent, and it turns out to be important, the interviewers are able flexibly to address this unanticipated matter.

A certain overlapping of responses and interview development can and did occur at any point in the interview. Ordinarily, the interview began with an innocuous question such as "When and where were you born?" and moved to questions about family and school.

A tandem interview is designed to maintain a conversational level in which the free flow of information can be assured. Interview situations invariably pose problems for the respondent. In a structured interviewer–interviewee, two-person arrangement, the respondent offers only a minimum of information. Introducing a third person informalizes and conversationalizes the situation. Each of our interviews lasted at least two hours. In qualitative inquiry, it is of the first importance that respondents be given every opportunity to articulate their feelings, their perceptions and their ideas as fully as possible. It was with this as our primary objective that the tandem depth interview was developed and initiated.

Once the interview was recorded on tape, a complete, verbatim transcription was printed. Then, after several careful readings, the data were classified and the analysis proceeded. In each category we examined the whole range of responses, the "average" pattern and variations on it. In this way, we hoped to preserve the richness and the typicality of experience reported to us.

Four Poverty Institutions: Youth Perceptions 4

School

Whether chronically delinquent, occasionally delinquent, pre-delinquent, or nondelinquent, young people tend to discuss school in depressingly familiar terms. Their collective testimony, with predictable but insignificant exceptions, is an extended confirmation of most of the worst stereotypes to be found in popular literature. Thus, in New York:

> The teachers are bad. I can do better playing hookey than going to P.S. ———.
>
> They just talk and talk — and when they tell you to do something, the bell rings.
>
> If you don't understand something, the teacher doesn't give you a chance to try again. He doesn't explain nothing.
>
> You know, they just yell at the class. It be hot and you be sticky. The class do something wrong, we be talking. They come in yelling. If they get in a bad mood and they don't want to be bothered with kids, they be yelling. They sit there and say they getting paid so it's okay if you don't want

to work. I just had to get out. I let somebody else take my seat. [This from a dropout who at first professed to have liked school and to have learned a lot there.]

There are youngsters who do not disparage their teachers; most can remember one or two who were excellent and who are esteemed because "they really taught us something," or because "they were really interested." More often, a good teacher is understood to be one who refrains from violence, who acts pleasant, cannot be easily ruffled, uses no foul language, or in a rare instance, actually fraternizes with his pupils, invites some of them to his home, buys them sodas, and the like. These are amiable characteristics, although they have no necessary connection with effective pedagogy. One may doubt, at least, that her English teachers taught much to the girl who says of all her teachers that: "They was good. They was nice with me."

There is bitter criticism — not always correlated with academic failure — and there is unqualified praise — not always correlated with academic success. Either way, it is hard to avoid a powerful sense of inadequacy. Hearing constantly that with diligence and intelligence, they "can make it in school," and seeing that few do, they are given to rote repetition of formulas like: "If you want to learn, you'll learn; if you don't want to, you won't" (from a "success," inordinately bright and alone in our sample destined for college, with a choice of scholarships), and "No, the schools are good. Nothing's wrong with them. The kids, they don't want to learn. They just don't bother to learn" (from a markedly less bright counterpart of the other who dropped out of school and bore illegitimate children).

On the surface, most respondents are able to tell us about the positive value of schooling. In our Washington sample, to the questions: "What is school for?" or "Why should children go to school?" they answer within the framework of standardized educational and vocational goals:

It helps you to get a job.

To give you a good idea of the outside world.

It helps you learn, to understand things that are happening out in the world today.

To get an education so you can get a decent job.

Yet, despite apparent understanding of what schools are *supposed* to accomplish, these young people (who range from the successful pupil to the hopeless dropout) tend to see the school as a penal institution which is at once obstacle course and battlefield. When they narrate their experiences and voice their complaints, the teacher–student relationship becomes central, specifically because it concerns how the teacher dispenses information and how the student incorporates knowledge.

Whatever the causes — how much the individual and how much the system are at fault — one finds a generalized state of demoralization. Pupils view school officials as hostile, indifferent, once in a while — but exceptionally and unpredictably — "nice," *and* also as people who, whether or not they "care," have pretty much given up on them. With feeble motivation in the first instance, large numbers give up on themselves.

One student in Washington, who repeatedly indicated his boredom and irritation at having to attend school, but was not yet a dropout, told us:

In shop, we'll be there for two hours — the whole afternoon just about. And all we do is talk to each other while he [the shop teacher] is outside doing something with another teacher. He gives us a test and that's our grade. In math, you might get enough — sometimes more than enough. In physics, the teacher go all out of her way. In art, you know if you put something down on paper and it don't look right, the teacher come and tell you it look right anyway. You know, in English, you don't learn enough and the teacher put you out for little odd things.

In consequence, some students can hardly remember when they did not play hookey. The first grader who has recently arrived from San Juan not knowing a word of English, when thrust into a classroom run by non-Spanish speakers, will be totally bewildered, quickly offended, and ripe for truancy. Presently, playing hookey implies more than just staying away from school. There is time for killing time, playing, "fooling around," by and by, sexual experimentation, fighting, stealing, "blowing pot," and finally various forms of narcosis, especially televiewing.

Playing hookey, then, can become a satisfying way of life which requires no dissimulation before adult interviewers. We ask: "Is it a lot of fun to play hookey?" Answer: "Yes." Question: "Is it more fun than going to school and learning?" Same answer. And why not? This youngster had helped to create an informal organization of boys and girls whose meeting place was established on a roof: "So any time somebody would play hookey, he knew they were up on the roof where they hang out. So we used to go up there. We always find somebody."

Similarly, in Washington, the standard response to boredom is to play hookey, and many fail to attend school as often as twice a week. On "days off," boys and girls organize parties and dances, or wander the streets looking for a "good time" until they can return without their parents being aware of the misdeed.

The youth of all three study areas share a truancy response to school conditions. Yet, in New York, going to a "pot party" is most frequent while totally absent in Chicago and Washington. In Washington, going to parties occurs most often. And in Chicago, racing cars and beer parties are the most common activities. As a result, delinquencies associated with school absenteeism can be expected to vary considerably between the three areas.

School, being a drag — where the price of perseverance "leading to a good job" is high and deemed by many a slum child to be too high — there are abundant attractions on the outside. Youngsters come together, usually in small groups in parks and on rooftops, and there disport themselves throughout the day as they do throughout much of the night, with such hedonistic pleasures as are available to them. But, of course, this is an outlaw way of life which can only produce conflict with parents, teachers, principals, administrators, cops, and judges. Yet, hookey, surely a real school problem, seems minor when contrasted to more serious incidents of conflict between teacher and student.

One incident, as a Washington youth recalls it, gives us some notion of the degree of antagonism between teacher and student:

> He [the teacher] put his hands on me and make me do something. I don't think that was right. I don't think a school is allowed to do that. It's supposed to be a janitor's job to pick up the paper. I don't think I'm no janitor, picking up paper for nobody. If he actually seen me throw the paper, I would have picked it up, see.
> [He didn't ask you very nicely?]
> No, he just said, "Charley, get out of line." Then he told me to stand over there by the window, you know. Then after awhile he said, "Pick that paper up." I said, "For what?" He said, "I seen your arm shoot that paper outside the hall." I said, "You ain't seen me shoot no paper." Then he said, "Get down there and pick that paper up." Then he grabbed me by the arm and tried to get me down there and pick that paper up. And I hit him.

And in Chicago, a chronic truant faced with entering high school describes his depression, especially in the face of inadequate preparation for this educational step:

> I didn't want to. None of the boys did. We didn't have no choice. Just about every one of us couldn't read worth shit.

An alternative for the basically dissatisfied child, lacking confidence in himself and in surroundings that seem to him to be penal, is to stay — and fight. He fights other children, which causes him to be disciplined. He also strikes out at authority, directly at teachers and other school officials, who strike back. The school becomes an arena of hostile forces with violence lurking in the background, and not infrequently coming to the fore. Some New York vignettes:

> This teacher, Mr. B., caught ahold of my brother, and boy, he gave him a good three slaps
> [for playing hookey].

> Mr. G., one day he punched me and I fell on the other side of the classroom. So I threw a chair at him.

The teacher had on this new coat and they ruined it on her and gave me the blame . . . I didn't do it. I got called down to the Dean's office. He asked me why did I do it? And I told him I didn't do it. But since I was a new girl in the class, there was no doubt . . . And then there was a radio stolen and they gave me the blame for that too.

Like I got in trouble with a teacher and she scratched me because I was holding the door, the outside door. I wouldn't let her out with the class. And then I ran out and when she came out, and she did like that [gesticulating] and I told her, "You better watch your nails." So I was going down the stairs and she said, "Your mother."
[Your mother?]
Yes. She called my mother a name. So I said, "Your mother etc."

I cursed at a teacher, a man teacher. I was jingling my bracelet, and he said something and I cursed at him, and he put me out of class.

Mr. W., he's my special teacher. When he loses his temper, he ain't like other teachers. Right away he goes hitting on people, picking on them, and then he blames it on the guys and girls.

[Did you ever see a kid hit a teacher?]
Yeah. One day he hit Mr. L. and Mr. L. didn't even put a finger on him, and I got mad and I just hit the boy. Mr. L., you know, me and him were close friends. He like me and I liked him. So when the guy hit him, I hit the guy back . . . Yeah, I got into trouble for that. The principal told me not to get into their business no more, but I couldn't help it.

She pinched me [allegedly for throwing a thumb tack].
[And you hit her? Where?]
In the face.
[Hard?]
Yeah.
[And what happened then?]
She fell down.

A Chicago youth, sensitive and talented, clinging marginally to school, verbalizes his predicament. Occasionally he "gets into gang fights," and is regarded by the school authorities as a troublemaker, partly because of his wit and an attendant ability to "put down" other boys. He reflects insightfully about the student–teacher relationship:

> I just want to make my point clear that I don't think the teachers in school are teaching the way they should. Because of their . . . desire for money. They teach for money, and not to teach the kids. If a slow student don't get it, that's his tough luck. The teachers tell us that they'll get paid whether we learn or not.

Between the habitual truants and the violent children who stay in school (and neither of these categories is sex- or age-specific), there are the apathetic who sit and stare and daydream their school days away. These may be as troubled as the obstreperous youth, but their quiescence provokes little antagonism. They are not likely to be sent to a "600 School," New York's special institution for "disturbed children" which one of its matriculants described to us as "worser than the Youth House" where he had been officially incarcerated. He added, "The teachers beat you up." And, "The Dean, Mr. L., is always hitting people. When you bring your mother in, he always talks nice." From his own experience:

> When I first came to that school, I was walking down the hall, minding my own business, and one of my friends came up and hit me on the back and I say, "Okay, I'm going to get you at three o'clock." And he [the Dean] grabbed me in his office and started hitting me with an iron ruler. I didn't say nothing. So he kept on, almost every time he seen me, you know. It's no school. It's a prison.

A Chicago dropout, recognizing his educational shortcomings, states:

> I don't know. I feel like I lack something. I don't know why. Just like somebody that wakes up in the morning; he's got a whole bunch of stuff. He lost one thing, but he can't figure out what it is, but yet he knows he lost it. Don't make much sense, but it's the only way I can put it.

The result of these school problems is objectively measured by the large number (and high rate) of dropouts. Why do they think school has so little holding power? Economic need, getting a job and helping the family, and pregnancy are important, but subordinate in their minds to apathy induced by conflict. These findings sharply clash with social scientific explanations which place heavy emphasis on such "causes" as emotional disorder and low intelligence. How these factors are related to the structure and operation of slum school systems has only been dealt with impressionistically.

Work

That poverty is self-perpetuating in the New York population under study became abundantly apparent whenever we ventured into questions of work with our respondents. It is clear, for instance, that for virtually all these people the range of gainful employment is exceedingly narrow. Low educational achievement is the first barrier. Parents and youngsters alike have had jobs in the marginal industries of New York — unprotected by minimum wage legislation or by union representation.

Every kind of menial job, as often institutional as private, and not much else, seems to be available to residents of East Harlem. Wages paid for such jobs leave the head of a household with children still in need of — and qualified for — relief. Men, women, and children can find work, although a surprising proportion of them do not know how to go about looking for it. The interviews reveal that specially organized agencies have failed to make any appreciable impact upon jobseekers, who have only a vague awareness, if any, of their existence. In all three study areas, newspaper ads and personal intervention by no more than two or three intermediaries on the block steer people to the job market more effectively than formal organizations set up for that purpose.

Repeated assertions that considerable schooling is necessary for the acquisition of skills, without which one cannot survive economically, have filtered down to the lowest strata of our society. Thus, asked why it is hard for him to find a job, a young man answers: "Because I don't have, I don't know, the training." Essentially, their explanation for not finding or keeping a job emphasizes their own ineptitudes or inadequacies. First, they say they do not have the necessary qualifications for good work — and for this, *they* are to blame. Or, they do not "try hard enough" on the job and therefore are "let go." In response to a question about the difficulties in obtaining work, one youth says: "It depends. Well, in my case, I wasn't really trying. Let's say I was shooting too high. My grandfather told me I would have to crawl before I walked, which I have done. So I say it all depends on the person."[1] Level of decency in income also has something to do with the prevailing attitude. So, among the employed there is an enormous turnover, usually justified on the basis that the pay was "rotten," "not enough," "lousy."

One Washington youth, actively seeking stable employment, relates the following experiences:

> [How many jobs have you been fired from?]
> Well, let's say . . . This job with the florist shop — the man said he let me go because, you know, he didn't think I'd work up to the standard. You may call that being fired. And I was in . . . When I was in high school, I work way out in Tacoma Park, Maryland as a bagger. And they had new management. They had new records on everybody and the man did have this staff overstaffed. So he said he had to let me go because he had hired too many boys, you know. We were working different shifts. So these are the only two jobs that I was let go, so to speak. You may call it firing, but I don't know. So I was told I was let go, but I'd consider it being fired.

The same youth worked as a bagger, helper, clerk–typist, messenger, and porter, all within a period of two years.

Job placement covers almost everything in this occupational universe whose locus is not limited to laundries, hospitals, and factories. The list includes short-order cooks, loaders, trimmers, female servants, hospital attendants, messengers, car washers, lifeguards, nurses' aides, teachers' aides, janitors, pressers, shipping

[1] A more complete analysis of this process and its consequences is developed in Chapter 8, Levels of Aspirations and the Ideology of Success.

clerks, waitresses, box makers, food dispensers (in the Welfare Department), dressmakers, butcher boys, parking lot attendants, stackers and packers, and male house cleaners — nearly all toiling part-time or full-time, but irregularly, with subsistence possible only when there is multiple employment within a single family unit. This means that children are likely to make small sums of money as baby sitters, delivery boys, and shoeshiners, or by "helping" in a retail establishment.

Similarly, in Washington, occupational placement was invariably menial and relatively unskilled. The young worked as porters, truck drivers, busboys, baby sitters, domestics, and low-level clerks. Every boy we questioned had been employed at one time or another. However, job turnover was enormous. Explanations of voluntary departure from a job most often centered upon monotony and low pay. In addition, since they are concentrated in marginal employment, whenever economic circumstances dictate these teenagers find themselves among the first to be "let go." In Chicago, the job market consists mainly of factory work. For younger males, the employment is semiskilled, unskilled or manual labor. Older males may become machine operators, drill pressers, spot welders, and general assembly-line workers. Their juniors are much more likely to be stock clerks or shipping clerks.

That wives work out of economic necessity, as many observers have noted, is a cause of destabilization in the Puerto Rican–American family. When that family remains intact, it may still be a point of pride for the Puerto Rican husband that his wife stays at home, as is evidenced in this comment of a young Puerto Rican husband: "I'm the man. She's the woman. She's not supposed to be working. I give her money to buy clothes on the weekend." (A more exotic touch is provided by the boy who reports that his grandmother's profession is to sit in houses of mourning as a spiritist, and that this function is fairly remunerative.)

One precollege girl has had much experience doing manual labor which is her temporary lot, ironically because she *is* a precollege girl:

> Well, I have muscles, calluses on my hands. I've been everything from a person who lifts watermelons onto trucks. I used to do men's jobs, since they're the only ones I could get since I'm

considered unskilled because I have an academic course and I'm not prepared for anything else. I stacked and packed in a record factory. I was an artist's model for awhile but I wasn't very good because it was quite strenuous. Figure modeling — where you stand and hold a position. Like if your arm is up in the air, you feel it straining but you still hold it because if you dare move, the artist says, "Look what you're doing, kid."

How much satisfaction work generally yields to these youth is roughly measured in this exchange:

[Which is the work you like best?]
I've only had three jobs.
[Which did you like best?]
None of them.

Chicago factory jobs are often described as "boring," "too hard," "too heavy," "too dirty." And getting to work without a car often is self-defeating since the worker quits before he can amass enough money to buy one. Public transportation is stigmatized. Occasionally low pay is deemed adequate, even good, but then there are other hazards. Satisfied with fifty dollars a week paid to her for trimming in a factory, one young lady found her income cut in half suddenly: "It got slow, real slow, and I used to go half-days. Sometimes they used to tell me to go home 'cause there was no work." And in one case, the specter of automation is raised. Asked whether with training he could get a job, an interviewee replied: "No, not these days. These days they got all those stupid machines. They're throwing everybody out." How accurate or prescient he is remains to be seen, but it goes without saying that this boy comes closer to the mark than most of his fellows.

The informal practices of getting work in the three areas are differently structured. In Chicago, where factory work is widely sought and highly prized (the principal reason for migrating from rural Appalachia), the network of information about job availability is more highly organized. It is a prime topic in daily conversation among peers. In New York and Washington, the process is much more haphazard, partly because work and knowledge of employment possibilities are more easily obtained through the daily newspapers, and partly because the matter is considered a highly personal and individual affair. Though all three groups are marginal in the world of work, they approach the common problem in their own way.

Welfare

Given the marginal employment and income circumstances of these poverty groups, welfare aid becomes a natural constituent of community life. If, at the time of our inquiry, almost one-third of the families were receiving assistance, still, among the youth in our New York sample, not one is "welfare-oriented" in the sense that he would prefer relief to work. We suspect that there may be a generational factor here, making adults more receptive to the welfare idea than their offspring — which, if true, would suggest that the voluntary perpetuation of poverty, with state-supplied subsistence, will not last indefinitely for large segments of the population. At the same time, as they report it, these young people belong to families a number of which either have never been on welfare or go on and off the welfare rolls in accordance with changing circumstances. Nor is there any perceptible relationship between welfare dependency and delinquent behavior. Whether the youngster's family is or is not on relief appears to tell us nothing else about him.

David Matza, in *Delinquency and Drift*,[2] has much to say about juvenile "sounding" in slum areas. The phenomenon is fairly complicated, but "sounding" is approximately peer-group "razzing" or "ragging" so extreme, provocative, and public as to cause humiliation. Nowhere else in our interviews is sounding as insistently discussed as it is in relation to welfare. One boy with an aunt on welfare has both sounded and been sounded about welfare — which he heartily dislikes because it engenders malicious gossip, almost always directed at one's mother, who, in a high proportion of cases, is one's only parent and protector. He speaks of the following barbs flung at a welfare child: "Your mother sells shopping bags on the corner. Your mother got hit by the rain. Your

---

[2] David Matza, *Delinquency and Drift* (New York: John Wiley and Sons, 1964), pp. 42–44.

mother's a truck driver." The reference may be made only in fun, but such sounding occasionally leads to fights. Beyond (and sometimes with) the sex-segregated peer group, they produce acute embarrassment. When emanating from schoolteachers or policemen, as is sometimes the case, they are construed as seriously degrading. Adolescent boys conceal their welfare status whenever possible from the world at large, but especially from girls, and vice versa.

In Washington, we asked:

> [Do kids usually tease other kids whose parents are on welfare?]
> No. I ain't never seen them tease nobody.
> Sometimes they joke about it.
> [What do they say?]
> C'mon, I know you're tired of eating those welfare beans, and all that.
> [What do you tell them?]
> Tell them to go to hell.

That children are highly sensitive to this form of social reprobation is unquestionable. Jibes, used as a device to gain advantages in competition or conflict, closely parallel those heard in New York. "At least my mother doesn't get that welfare food." "At least my mother isn't on welfare." And so on.

Consequently, the negative evaluation of welfare among these teenagers (and it is not wholly negative) has much more to do with shame, a condition induced by the moral judgment of others, than with guilt, a condition induced by the breach of internalized norms. In short, the moral commitment to work is not nearly as strong as the fear of censure for having to accept welfare. The teasing and joking and "making fun" of welfare people is hard enough to bear. It may come out like this: "What did you have? Rice? Cheese? Beans?" Such banter can produce relatively painless give and take. The publicity attendant upon accepting free lunches in school or simply securing welfare food seems to inflict a deeper hurt. Neighbors taunt a girl receiving public assistance for herself and her illegitimate child by saying that she cannot afford to buy things and she retaliates with, "One of these days you'll be on welfare too," — which seems to give her only limited satisfaction.

In these circumstances, it becomes difficult to maintain a reasonable attitude toward welfare. The confusion and pathos which follow are revealed in this series of questions and answers:

[Well, you get welfare money. Do you think that's a good thing?]
No.
[Why?]
You don't get enough. Like my teacher, my new guidance teacher, he says that being on welfare is no good.
[Why?]
I don't like when he say that. He don't embarrass me because my mother takes welfare, but he embarrass other people.
[Why are you ashamed of getting welfare?]
Sometimes some guys in my class take welfare, and one guy asks, "You take welfare?" Sometimes I say, "Why don't you like it? You know, they support you. They won't let you die . . . " I tell 'em, "Those are people that worry about you. They like to help you out."
[What do the kids say?]
They start cursing at them like that. Some of them have a ball — when they need money for graduation, like that. The teacher say, "Where's your graduation money?" They say, "The check hasn't come."

The shame of being a welfare recipient can also be seen as a factor inhibiting those families in need from making application for assistance. Rejecting welfare while needing it may be their last resort in maintaining human dignity. To become a permanent public charge is to lose hope and suffer untold humiliation. An astute Washington adolescent sums up:

Well, see, the people that are poor and don't take welfare, you know, they got a little pride to 'em. And the people who are poor and do take welfare, I mean they got pride but they have to push it back. They're in need. Pride ain't nothing when it comes down to that. I mean, the average man would push back his pride, and take on a given hand. I would.

A few individuals are deeply aggrieved over welfare policy. Thus, an unwed mother exclaims: "That welfare! I'm going to sue if they don't send me money. They're crazy." Too young to receive her own check, she is part of her mother's welfare case, but receives a supplementary allotment of seventeen dollars a week for her child. She wonders: "What am I going to do with $17? The milk I get her cost twenty-nine cents. She drinks a can and a half every day. Baby food. What am I going to do with $17? What I buy her is more than $17. I have to buy stuff for me too . . . I have no clothes. What am I going to do?" Another youngster, asked if his mother complains about the social investigator, replies:

> No, she just says some of them are very nasty. Like this new one, this guy, he really makes me laugh at his statement. My mother said, "He said this place had the look of a poorhouse." And I mean, my mother, she didn't know what to say. It was so funny. She started to ask him, "Well, darn it, if we were rich, do you think we'd be on welfare?" Some of them say the most outlandish stupid things.

Here the hostility is deflected onto specific obtuse caseworkers.

In Chicago, the anger is most open and direct. A girl whose large family receives public assistance complains:

> [What is your opinion of welfare caseworkers?]
> I don't like them. They might say, "I'll try to help you. I'll try to do this and I'll try to do that," but that's just like saying something you memorized. It doesn't have any meaning at all. Well, our family is on welfare and I know many times we didn't have any money in the house or anything and it was really terrible because they held the check up.
> [How do you feel about being on welfare?]
> I don't like it one bit. Being on welfare, well, you don't earn the money yourself. To me, it's just a downgrade. It's just taking charity. If you really are unable to work, then I think welfare is nice. I mean, it comes in handy. But my dad was too lazy to work, and I think they knew it too. There could have been something wrong, but I doubt it very much. It was

one of those cases. It takes away your . . . Well, I know it took away *my* pride.

Another Chicago youth:

[What do you think of caseworkers?]
I don't like them. Sometimes they're mean. Sometimes they'll yell at you and try to make you confess to something you didn't do. They come out and they try to say that your mother don't take good care of her kids or something.
[What do you think about being on welfare?]
I hate it 'cause you never get freedom. Never get enough money to go places. And if my mom can't come out to see John [institutionalized, mentally retarded] or something, they start yelling and throwing fits, and Mom tells them, "All right, I haven't got the money. My checks don't come on time."

[Is welfare something to be ashamed of?]
Sometimes, because you don't have enough money to live on, but you live. Well, on our block, for instance, you know where there's that building # ——? Well, my mom had just gone down and when she came back, her welfare worker had been there and just really cussed my brother out. She was so stupid. I mean, you know, she blames him for stuff he didn't do and says, "Well, why can't you clean up this house a little bit?" And he says, "Well, I been busy trying to fix the kids lunch so they can go back to school on time, and I been trying to watch after my younger brother and trying to get everything done."
[Do you think it will be possible for you not to be on welfare when you're older?]
Yes, I do. I don't care how much I hate school. *I'm not gonna be on welfare.*

It's dependent and I hate to be dependent. They're all the time on to you about this or that. Like you have a buddy spend the night with you. The welfare finds out, they give you all kinds of hell for that.
[Do they ask your mother if she's got a boyfriend?]
Yes sir, boy, and if they catch him, they cut off the welfare.

Such gripes and those of a more general, abstract nature are rather frequent in this area.

Much more common is the sense of embarrassment caused by "getting on line and having people look at you," an experience which gets to be truly excruciating if you are a teenage boy and "a girl watches you getting food from the Welfare Department." Then, "You're dead. You're in deep trouble, man! She won't even date you for nothing!" If you should let somebody know you're on welfare and he is not completely trustworthy (sometimes cliques of "welfare boys" form, sharing the secret they more or less vainly seek to conceal), then "That guy lay it on you. Then they'll get us together, all the friends and everything — and laugh at us."

Perhaps in a society where self-help and individual effort are regarded as the prime sources of economic and social stability, any form of "welfare dependency" will be interpreted by both individual and community as a mark of failure. However, to those we interviewed, no other type of public aid (be it economic, social, or educational) signifies as much as welfare.

There is, of course, much more to the welfare story than we have indicated. This much suffices, however, to make clear that it arouses strong feelings — and, incidentally, casts a bright light on the internal structure of social control in a contemporary slum.

Police

A New York street whose local and national reputation is that of the "worst and most crime-ridden block" can be expected to feel the full impact of police activity. A casual observer of our New York study block witnesses policemen standing either at one corner or the other, on course in solitary patrol, merely looking about, amiably chatting with a resident, stolidly going about their business. This activity is a daily occurrence whether or not crimes are known to have been committed. In contrast, those of us more familiar with middle-class community life would not expect a regular encounter with policemen who are omnipresent in urban slums.

They are bound to play a significant role in the community,

their shields and nightsticks an ever-visible, active force of community existence.

The situation in Washington is quite different. Patrolmen in the D.C. study area, save for an occasional foray through the streets, are rarely visible. Even more rarely are they active participants in the daily life of the community.

One youth claims: "As long as I can remember, I never seen but one cop pass my house. And I seen, you know, about three of them going past in a scout car. That's as long as I can remember. Now I can't say what they were doing or what they might be." Another youth, a self-admitted chronic deviant, elaborates: "Only time the police are there is to come in after it happened. Very seldom they're there when it happens. Okay, you've got all those policemen around there. Maybe one time a week. Now where are they the rest of the time? I have beat many people up and took their money out in the street. Where was the police?"

Certainly, it is clear that police impact upon youth and other community members will vary considerably whenever the role of the patrolmen differs from one area to another. The police role in a given community need not be contingent upon the actual frequency or real magnitude of lawbreaking. Considerations other than incidence of crime and delinquency may well determine the manner in which police officers are employed throughout an urban area.

Both technological factors and available police resources play a significant role in the deployment of police. Although the question of why and how official administrative policies develop is not central to our study, careful account must be kept of variations in practice from city to city.

The advantage of a cross-cultural perspective is that it helps to explain a spectrum of human response to apparently identical or similar social conditions. Thus, youth in Washington appear to have little direct knowledge of or experience with police. Their answers are typically sparse except in those cases where they have been apprehended, arrested, molested, or otherwise directly processed by police officers.

In Chicago, residents see more patrol cars; at least one passes by every fifteen minutes. Chicago police no longer walk beats; they view the scene from their squad cars.

Youth reared and now living in the study block were systematically questioned about their experiences and relationships with the police. At first, a majority of them balked and refused to discuss the topic. When pressed, their answers were evasive and superficial. Stimulating them to discuss illicit behavior proved to be easier than probing their attitudes toward policemen. Regular requestioning did, however, give us a picture of interaction more subtle than, and often starkly in contrast with, contemporary images — according to which policemen and slum dwellers live in mutual disdain and daily conflict.

We were able to distinguish three different types of response which went beyond vague references to "police brutality," and "police corruption." Did the police use physical force unnecessarily when involved in an arrest or even when they merely suspected that a crime had been committed? Were the police honest? Did our respondents ever see a cop take a payoff? We wanted to ascertain whether the interviewee (1) actually experienced or perceived an occurrence, or (2) simply relayed secondhand information, or (3) maintained a belief about police activity without being able to indicate its actual source.

We received all three types of response, with or without independent verification. Yet, if a single theme emerged from the interviews, it was this: that police–community relations exist in a condition of mutual *accommodation* and not nearly so much in a state of potential *conflict.*

Many examples of police corruption and brutality (based either on experience or second-hand information) were presented to us. But our respondents rationalized these beliefs with elaborate apology for the police. They offered the apology despite their ambivalence, which prompted them to say that they do not like cops, most of whom are "mean and crooked" — and then led them to state that they understand the difficulties of police work.

This habitual mixture of feelings is expressed by a New York boy whose family has often been caught up with the police. His response begins with an apology:

> [Do you think cops are cruel? Unfair?]
> They're doing the best of their ability. What they think is the best. Just like, for example, you're an officer and you think

this boy is going to pull out a gun on you. You're going to take it out and shoot first. You, after all, you're an officer or you become something. You use it to the best of your ability when you have a job. Like a teacher or as a doctor, you do what you think is best.

[Do you know boys who have been victims of police brutality?]

Yes I do.

[Were you?]

Never. My brother was.

[What happened?]

Well, he was put away in a penitentiary because he did something against the law. Then he planned to escape. But during the escape, he surrendered. And the cops deal with him very badly. Put him in critical condition. Not as far as I understand that. Once you surrender, they're not supposed to beat you up and they did it. Now it's true that you can't fight City Hall. But through a beating like this, when a person becomes a maniac, it's a memory you can't forget.

[It affected his mind?]

No, not to that point. Right now he seems very well. I hope that taught him a lesson.

[Did they beat him over the head?]

They beat him on the body. They did not beat him on his head because that probably would have killed him. But they beat him with rubber nightsticks.

Here, the respondent, though clearly aware of police brutality, nevertheless shifts from apology to anger to apology during the course of his commentary.

Frequently, when asked whether they believe cops are honest, respondents reply in the negative. Nevertheless, almost in the same breath, they justify police dishonesty (whether witnessed by them or simply as something they heard about) with the classical rhetorical excuse: "If you were in their shoes, wouldn't you?"

Similarly, in Washington, a good deal of ambivalence is apparent. For example:

[Are there dishonest cops?]

Yeah.

[Why do you say that?]
Well, some of them, you know, do just like regular people do. You know, some of them honest, some of them dishonest.

Some show their anger more openly:

I don't think all policemen are out to help people because some, they might know where a gambling place is or people selling dope. And people give them enough money and they won't say anything about it. I don't think they're better than anybody else.

In Chicago, the attitude is less ambivalently negative. One sixteen year old states: "They're good at times, but if you don't want 'em, when you're swiping something, then they come around. If you need 'em, like for gang fights, they're nowhere." And another: ". . . They ain't no good, always messing up everything. Especially when they catch you. [Otherwise they] treat us all right . . . They threaten that they're gonna beat you up. They just talk, just want to scare you."

In addition, the "nice cop" or "good cop" is not necessarily equated with the "honest cop" or the "kind cop." One policeman who enjoys the reputation of being a "good cop" was also described as tough and much given to the arbitrary use of physical force. These respondents consistently emphasized the personal performance, the style of an officer, rather than whether he chronically moved beyond the bounds of proper police activity.

Above all, the police are perceived as requiring that they be treated respectfully, at least on the surface, in day-to-day confrontations:

[Did you ever have a friendly conversation with a cop?]
I don't even tell 'em "Hi." Mostly you gotta call a cop "officer" when you say hello. So I say, "Hello, cop." And he says, "What?" Then I say, "Officer." That guy got me embarrassed, so I never call him cop no more; only to tell him, "Hi. How you doing? Drop dead."

Unquestionably, police brutality and police corruption do exist. Whether they are persistent patterns or isolated incidents is, for our present purposes, a secondary consideration. More important is the tenacious *belief* that official agents of social control go beyond the bounds of propriety. It is in this context of amorality, if not immorality, that an accommodation occurs. When, as we shall argue, moral anomie prevails within a community, this factor becomes a more significant aspect of the total social configuration. For when agents of law and order, those visible representatives of the conventional world, are perceived as unconventional and deviant, then youth possessed of these conceptions become less than certain in distinguishing between clear-cut categories of right and wrong, good and bad.[3]

From these perceptions of youth in each community, three basic conclusions seem indicated:

1. Although the major social institutions in each study area bear marked similarities both in fact and in perception (thus lending a measure of credence and substantiation to the notion of a culture of poverty), there also emerges significant institutional and cultural variability in each of these communities.
2. One vector of cultural variability has as its source the traditional elements of the different communities (that is, ethnicity, nativity).
3. Another source of cultural variation is located in the variations in the structure and organization of community life (that is, housing arrangements, size of population, type of surrounding community).

As our material on sexual patterns, fighting, and stealing will suggest, cultural variability in turn determines significant variations in behavior patterns of those similarly located in the socioeconomic scale. Within the framework of our inquiry, these variable patterns focus along modalities of conformity-deviance and nondelinquency and delinquency.[4]

---

[3]See Chapter 9 for a more complete discussion of "moral anomie."

[4]This is not to suggest that deviance, in general, is necessarily overdetermined for a specific social category (the lower class) but rather that deviance is class-typed as well as culturally variable within and between social classes.

Patterns of Sexual Behavior 5

A common culture presupposes that those who belong to it speak the same language. There is such a language for all Americans as there is an overarching culture that unifies urban dwellers and farmers, the young and the old, the privileged and the underprivileged. Subcultural segmentation produces "special languages" within the larger linguistic community, and they are intelligible only to initiates, that is, members of ethnic, occupational, regional, and religious groups. That the broadly conceptualized culture (or subculture) of poverty is somewhat illusory can be demonstrated by the variegated speech patterns characteristic of poor Appalachian whites, Negroes, and Puerto Ricans. Indeed, for each of our populations it would be possible to assemble a glossary of terms, widely used by insiders but meaningless to most outsiders. How luxuriant local variation (in meaning, accent, and value) takes place is the proper subject matter of a highly technical discipline called ethnolinguistics. It is not our intention to turn that discipline loose on data gathered for other purposes. Nevertheless, this much must be said: each group living in its own slum moves toward a certain linguistic homogeneity, bringing ancestral speech ways, borrowing symbols from the larger society, and synthesizing them into distinctive configurations. Peculiarities of speech are a rough index of differential association and cultural isolation.

Unique idioms emerge from intense in-group living, and disappear at the opposite pole of full acculturation. In between, we find a complex mixture reflecting uneven exposure to the wider institutional order, which is itself in constant flux. A few illustrations from the heterosexual sphere may be in order.

In our sample, the adolescent males of New York and Washington are unresponsive to questions about dating. The word does not appear in their lexicon, and, as it turns out, this fact points to a substantive difference in behavior between these boys and those in Chicago. Every respondent in Chicago knows what a date is. One at first defines it as, "Goin' out with a fox," then adds, "you just go out driving, make some love, catch a crib — and that's all." Here indeed are the cadences, the inflections and the semantics of a special language in which "fox" means girl and "crib" stands for house or apartment, which in turn signifies a trysting place that one "catches" along with the "fox." Such expressions may have their origin in the hill country of Kentucky and Alabama, whence they were transplanted to the midwest and, merged with much else, produced a dynamic amalgam that cannot be duplicated elsewhere.

There are fuzzy edges around every word that is variously defined not only at different levels of the social hierarchy, but within any one level. For those who generalize in the grand manner, dating is understood to be "an American" phenomenon; the more sophisticated family sociologists who prepare textbooks for college students see it as a peculiar ritual, a courtship pattern, practiced by middle-class youth in the United States. In our samplings of the underclass, only teenagers in Chicago date, and they do so in ways similar to and dissimilar from those of their middle-class counterparts. The telephone for instance plays no great part in their activities, as it does among more privileged adolescents, but the automobile is central. Neither matters much in New York and Washington.

The Chicago boys, who will sometimes commit crimes to get a car and need it to commit other crimes, whose vocabulary is rich with the knowledge they have of car parts, may be said to live in a car complex. This circumstance provides them with a degree of physical mobility far greater than that of any other economically deprived group we have studied. In a crisis, occasioned, say, by the impregnation of a girl friend (by no means a rare occurrence), they can always take to the road, ranging widely over Illinois and adjacent states. The automobile liberates them, up to a point, not only from their constricted neighborhood, but from the metropolis itself. And, given the car, they are able to date girls in a more or less conventional manner. The "portable bedroom" can be used for preliminary sex play most conveniently at drive-in movies where two or three couples commonly occupy one car. Asked what he usually does on a date, a fifteen year old Chicago boy, replies in part:

> . . . If your friend's got a girl he's taking to the drive-in, you take her with him. And you take your girl to the show, go out to eat, dance, stuff like that. . . .

On the average, what does a date cost?

> Well, if you go to a show, you won't have to spend but about, at the most, five, maybe six dollars . . . If you go to the drive-in, you spend a dollar and a half for each one to get in. That's three dollars. Give the kid who's driving the car a buck, split the gas bill, you know, help to pay for some of the gas — and you eat. Oh, it costs you about six dollars.

Bowling and roller-skating are other diversions deemed to be suitable on dates in Chicago. Neither is a popular boy–girl pastime in the other cities — where boys like sports they play with other boys. Pickups are made on the street from a car, in neighborhood movie houses, and teenage bars which are frequented with great regularity only in Chicago.

All of this sounds a great deal like the textbook account, even to a general preference for double-dating. Yet, the reasons behind that preference give us a clue to something different and specific to the Chicago group, namely that a heavy streak of violence is woven into the texture of their heterosexual behavior. Hence: "I like to go out with other couples because it's better when you travel together. When you're alone, there's always other guys trying to start trouble." You date, but you appear alone with a girl at your own peril, as this little vignette makes clear:

> I saw her walking down the hall with another boy, and I got pretty jealous. I started saying, "If you like that guy so much, go ahead and go out with him," and he walked up and started smartin' off to me. So I hit him, and then I beat him up. She turned around and slapped me. She called me a brute or something . . . So that didn't hit me just right, and I said, "Forget it."

If a date culminates in sexual intercourse, it is also useful to have someone else along:

> I was going with a girl. She was sixteen. She squealed on me, and they tried to get me on statutory rape. And, oh, she gave 'em a big long story, trying to get me into a lot of trouble. But there was another kid along with me on that date. And she claimed that he held her down and that I held her down. But this boy's stories matched and hers didn't. Otherwise, I would have been sunk . . .

With dating, there go the lineaments of a rating–dating complex, which does not precisely parallel Willard Waller's famous description of a widespread campus phenomenon, but does imply a measure of respect for the girls one dates, by contrast with the disrespect accorded girls and older women who are nothing but sexual objects. The following example is somewhat extreme but highly indicative:

> I consider a girl you go out with and a girl you have intercourse with two different kinds of girls. There's a girl I date. I like to hold hands with her and make out with her, kiss her, but that's as far as I want to go with any girl I take out. If I like the girl, I don't want to mess her up. But then, there is the other girls I just don't care about because they give it to the other guys — which means they don't care too much for theirselves.

The type of boy who makes this provisionally puritanical division between good girls (with lovers who hold back from final consummation) and bad girls who "give it to the other guys," is yet capable of treating "good girls" with greater harshness than their fallen sisters. This double standard means that there are separate norms;

less is expected of the promiscuous girl, much more of the girl you date who may after all become your wife. If so, unquestioning submission to male authority is expected:

What if you married a girl who talked back to you? What would you do?
Shut her up.
How?
Well, I'd fix her where she wasn't able to talk too much. Smack!

The respecter of violence is omnipresent. It may issue from association with either type of girl, and although there are always two types, criteria for establishing them vary. (Asked whether he still considers girls decent if they go to bed with him, a Chicago boy answers, "It's a matter of how hard I have to work. If I have to work real hard I think a lot of them. If they give it to me right off I think they're pigs.") Infidelity in a girl friend will ordinarily provoke a physical assault of some sort. What to do if the woman you marry is unfaithful? "Beat the shit out of her," is the semi-automatic response.

Acts of aggression connected with sex no doubt are intensified by heavy consumption of alcohol. Sex, liquor, and violence form a gestalt in Chicago not nearly so discernible in New York or Washington. In another context, whiskey and beer act as a catalyst for serious fighting, possibly with recourse to knives and firearms. In the sexual context, alcohol is also believed to be useful in emboldening the boy and rendering the girl more compliant to his advances:

Do the girls get pretty wild when they've had a few drinks?
Yes.
Do most of the guys try to get the girls loaded?
Yes.
How often are you successful?
We're not very successful at getting them loaded. I mean that takes a little money.

Beer is cheaper than whiskey and favored for that reason; a low alcohol content notwithstanding, it is believed to serve the purpose. Girls plied with beer are considered "better," that is, more available, than those who remain unlubricated. They can more easily be "cut" — which is typical and revealing Chicago argot for the sex act.

In New York there is no "cutting." The first few interviews with Puerto Rican youth revealed little about sex, a topic concerning which we had not anticipated that there would be unusual reticence. The breakdown in communication turned out to be no more than terminological. Once in possession of key words and phrases, the interviewers encountered no serious resistance to the free discussion of plain and fancy sex. There are taboo topics, notably religion as it shades off into magic, but sex is not one of them. The linguistic breakthrough occurred in this matter when a resident observer advised us to ask about "scheming." We did so, causing faces to light up that had remained blank as long as we struggled vainly to find the right conventional or unconventional sexual expression. "Scheming" was that expression. Equivalent, in a way, to "cutting" which suggests sex-and-sadism, "scheming" had mildly conspiratorial overtones. It stands for kissing, necking, petting, and full sexual consummation, the whole gamut from prepubertal exploration to real coitus, which is secret, explorative, pleasurable, but seldom brutal. With appropriate language, much information can be elicited, and comic misunderstandings are left behind. (To the question, "Did you ever have a girl sexually?" respondent answers by asking, "Did I ever have a girl *sectionally?*" and some minutes are consumed, to no avail, in disentangling the adverbs. We want to know from another boy whether he goes to bed with girls, whether he sleeps with them, and he takes us literally: "No. I sleep by myself, in my own bed.")

Scheming is initiated at parties, and parties are called sets. They function as substitutes for going out, picking up, and dating. Young people at or around twenty may have apartments of their own which, like any of many vacant apartments on the block, can be used for sets, as they can be and are used for private or collective sexual adventures. Boys and girls meet at sets, play records, dance, drink beer or whiskey more or less moderately, smoke cigarettes, and take pot more or less immoderately, and under dim colored lights, engage in uninhibited foreplay. With twenty or more in attendance, sets seem to be fairly large affairs, and while some are organized during the week by hedonistic truants, there are sure to be others around the clock on weekends. Since the youngsters use stimulants and depressants that are costly, and Saturday is the traditional day for pilfering small objects whose sale produces money to buy supplies, the best sets are most likely to occur on Saturday nights. You drink a little, you smoke a lot, you are high, a girl offers to dance with you, and by and by when the dim lights go out altogether, you fondle her. Presently, you step outside with your girl, scheme in the hallway, at her place if no one is at home, on a rooftop, this one or another at the nearby housing project. And:

> If you got a really good friend, and the girl is willing if she's really bad off or somethin', you know what she will do? *She'll pull the train . . .*
> [Pull the train?]
> Yes, that's what we call it: pulling the train. You take one chance. Then another guy takes a chance. You know.
> [Usually, how many guys are there?]
> Two.
> [Not like ten guys with one girl?]
> Oh, depends like on what kind of girl . . . I been in a situation with about six guys.

"Pulling the train" is by no means an everyday occurrence. Sets are. They may be regarded as a spontaneous expression of youth culture, an informal device contrived by teenagers for their own pleasure, a technique for circumventing official and established organizations, an escape from uplift sponsored by benevolent adults. Sets provide an arena — or constitute a preparation — for scheming which, in most cases, means private and secret sexual activity. Boys do boast, with a probable admixture of fantasy and exaggeration, about sexual conquests, but they are loath to name names and thus cause "trouble" for themselves or their girlfriends. The set in which they begin to participate at about age fifteen is understood to be somewhat illicit. It may become a pot party or a sex party (our respondents are ambivalent and divided among themselves about which they like best) — and either one, if publicized, can lead to unpleasant sanctions.

Boy–girl relations in Washington are neither as car- and show-centered as in Chicago nor as party-centered as in New York. In Washington, the school, despite all its deficiencies, is much more pivotal than we would have supposed. Young people attend school dances now and then, meet classmates formally and informally, and, while ungoverned by any particular protocol, they begin to "go out" with one another. Soon there is sex play, and in many cases, real sexual involvement. Things tend to begin in school, and there, too, the "facts of life" are transmitted most frequently and most effectively. Only in our Washington sample do high school children use technical (now and then garbled) scientific terms for the sex act and the sex organs. They describe human reproduction as it has been explained to them by their biology teachers:

> We had it in school. I know how the sperms come down, when a boy is having sex relations with a girl; they meet the egg, go up through the vagina, stay in the womb and grow month after month. And then after a period of time, the woman have a baby. . . .
>
> We're supposed to do that next half, after we finish with music . . . find out where babies come from and things like that. . . .
>
> Well, I know the process of starting — I mean, you have to have two unions, I mean a fusion of, uh, male and female, between the two organs. I mean the vulva and the, um, penis. The vulva and the penis. And, um, it takes a union of sperm and meeting with the egg. And after that, I know the situation of — what do you call it? — the embry — yeah, embry — and that's the first stage of the child . . . And the food which the child receives comes from the navel of the mother. It's connected to the child, I believe mouth-to-navel, something like that. And after a nine month period, the child's supposed to be born. . . .

A boy whose parents told him "all about it" at age twelve, says:

> They explained it to me, that it was the entrance of the penis into the woman's vulva. I mean, they used other terms, but that's the terms I would use because, let's say, I'm more up on it now, on this education. . . .

Again:

> Well, uh, let's see, when the sperm, I think goes into the vagina,

something like that, then, it meets the other sperm I think, and it starts doing something. . . .

However imperfectly they may have absorbed their biology lessons, these teenagers show a degree of sophistication unavailable to their counterparts in New York and Chicago where sexual knowledge is more likely to be associated with the street — and its earthy language — than with the classroom. (In New York a self-taught, semi-demi-social worker has helpfully taken it upon himself to provide some sex instruction in yet another linguistic style, largely Spanish, partly English argot.) For children to seek or parents to offer information, even when it is urgently needed, seems to be a rare occurence. (We suspect that parent–youth embarassment on this score is a class phenomenon. There is reason to believe that the middle-class parent now speaks freely to his children about the facts of life while evading questions about the facts of death.) The young mother of two illegitimate children in Washington tells us that she developed early: "At the age of twelve I was as developed as any girl of fourteen or fifteen. Being young, I never paid too much attention to it, but other older people in the community noticed." As she recounts it, men got fresh, some began to follow her home and she took to making "smart" remarks, and then, after awhile, "I had one man run me home after school." She ran and found sanctuary on a neighbor's porch, and, "The man started to come after me till he looked up and spotted a lady and another man on the porch. After that my mother came over, and we told her about it, and the three of them walked around, but they didn't see him." This incident was but the first of several, including one "proposition" from a preacher, about which the mother was informed. She still divulged nothing to her daughter, and the daughter observes, "I just could not bring myself to look up at my mother and ask her what was happening." The whole story, "the nitty-gritty," came from experience with "fellows" who were judged to be stupid, however, as well as girls on the street and an older sister. From her own account, but never officially, she was a sexual delinquent by age thirteen.

On the other hand, in Washington, a boy may experience sexual initiation under his father's auspices. If there is an older woman who wishes to "come some," that is, who wishes to have a sex partner, the father sometimes encourages his son to cooperate. We have one such case on record:

> She [the older woman] came down to see my sister, and she started liking me. She started paying my way to the movies and all that. So my father told me to go on and do it. So I did . . . He say, "I know you going to do it when I ain't around." So he gave me a protector, and I go on and do it . . . He say we were going to do it behind his back anyhow, and that he just wanted to help me along. I ain't never used the protection, though. . . .

Although he tends to confuse protection against venereal disease with protection against pregnancy, the Washington teenager is generally more knowledgeable about this, too, than his age mate in New York and Chicago. He more often recognizes and applies terms like contraceptive, diaphragm, coil, prophylactic, or rubber — for one reason, because he more often knows what they mean. Not that he or his girlfriend is much inclined to use any of these objects, for their interposition threatens the individual with loss of his "cool" — an important but amorphous quality which must be maintained at all times. Although in all of the three cities only a minority favor contraception, Washington youth understand best, and New York youth least, just what it is they habitually decline to use. And, while amorality or *anomie* tends to prevail in sexual matters, it assumes a degree of egocentricity among Chicago boys unequaled elsewhere. In this exchange, we have an extreme but not a typical expression of the Chicago attitude:

> [Do you ever use contraceptives?]
> Nope.
> [How about women? Do they ever use anything?]
> Nope.
> [Do you ever think about it?]
> Nope.
> [Are you afraid of what might happen?]
> Nope. *They can't touch me. I'm underage.*

Seeing it exclusively from his own standpoint, and then only insofar as his conduct may lead to legal jeopardy, he is not afraid of making girls pregnant. Later on, when he does come of age, in order to avoid possible charges of statutory rape, such a boy will prefer sexual relations with older women. Even then, this respondent insists, he "ain't gonna use anything." Told by the interviewer about diaphragms and how they work, he vehemently protests against their use. They would interfere with his pleasure, "Might get in my way." To be sure, without contraception, it is possible to spawn an illegitimate child, something he at first claims to have done at least once — before second thoughts cause him to cast doubt on the "mother's" veracity. This is his complete verbatim statement on the matter:

> She told me we were gonna have a kid. I said, "Tough." She said, "Ain't it though?" I said, "What you gonna do about it?" She said, "I ain't gonna do nothin' about it. How about you?" I said nothin'. She said, "That's good." I said goodbye and she said goodbye. And that's the last I saw of her. I mean I *saw* her in school. She's still goin' to school. I don't believe that we had a kid, though. She just said we did.

Risk or no risk, boys are generally hostile to the idea of prophylaxis. One objection is phrased purely in terms of the pleasure principle, most colorfully by a Chicago boy who explains why he never uses anything like a rubber, "I tried it once. It's like riding a horse with a saddle instead of bareback." Is he afraid of "knocking a girl up?" Answer: "Sure. *I worry about it afterward.* I guess I'm lucky so far. That's all." The cost factor appears again in Chicago where boys are markedly more reluctant than in Washington and New York to spend money on contraceptive frills. At the climatic moment, their impecuniosity can be frustrating. As a rule in this population girls are no more eager than boys to insure against pregnancy, but once in awhile they are:

> Oh, I've used them a couple of times. Like one time, a broad got all worried, and she told us to lay off. . . . We had her pants off and everything. She ask me if I didn't have some rubbers. Uh-uh. "Get off." I had to wait a little longer. I didn't have any money either.

In Chicago there is, then, a minimum of anxiety about the consequences of sexual intercourse, a strong disinclination to take any responsibility for what happens. Most boys are poorly informed and unconcerned about measures taken or not taken by their sex partners. "I wouldn't know if they did or not [use anything to prevent pregnancy]. I don't care if they do or not." Does he know what girls might do to protect themselves? "Well, there's with the hot water, like that. Then, there's, they press on their stomachs someplace . . . on some cords, usually when you get done, the girl has to go to the bathroom. She goes in, she presses here and there, and it all comes out. They claim that's one of the best ways." Ignorance of the facts should not be discounted, but knowledge may or may not be correlative with action. Even if a girl asks for restraint, so that she will not have to cope with unwed motherhood, the boy is likely to refuse:

[Do many girls ask you to stop before you come?]
Most don't. Some do.
[They don't want to get pregnant?]
That's right.
[Do you usually oblige them?]
Well, not usually, no.

Anatomists like Ashley Montagu have established the existence of adolescent sterility, a period after the onset of puberty during which reproduction presumably cannot take place.[1] Widespread premarital sexual experimentation, not always related to courtship, among "primitive peoples" to whom puritanism is unknown, has been noted for over a century. Adolescent sterility helps anthropologists to account for the smoothness with which such relations occur. In ever-larger sectors of our own society, birth control has "sterilized" teenagers, thereby insuring them against the many complications of illegitimacy. Neither of these mechanisms seems to be significantly operative in any of our cities. Adolescent *fertility* is high, and respondents (males only slightly more so than females) express a very nearly uniform distaste for every kind of contracep-

---

[1] Ashley Montagu, *Adolescent Sterility: A Study in the Comparative Physiology of the Adolescent Organism in Mammals and Man* (Springfield, Illinois: C. C. Thomas, 1946).

tive device. Significant differences are in the first instance more attitudinal than behavioral. How much responsibility does a boy feel when he has got his girl with child? Some in New York and Washington; virtually none in Chicago. That unimpeded sexual contact can and does lead to babies is something a transplanted Appalachian white boy is likely to know only too well. For the most part, "He couldn't care less"; the interviewer asks such a boy: "What's stopping you from knocking up girls?" Answer: "Nothin'. I've got four kids, maybe five. Two here in Chicago, two in Wisconsin, and when I left Wisconsin, I heard there was one more." Does he support any of them? "Shit, no." After getting a girl pregnant, "I just take off."

Less able to "take off," as carefree but more likely to be careless, hemmed in on every side, the New York boy generally finds insemination of his girlfriends a worrisome matter. It is seldom a question of direct responsibility to the "victim" — which would presuppose a kind of socialization or internalization of standards evident neither among "good boys" nor among "bad boys." What if the girl has a baby? "Maybe the parents might make him marry her." Coercion under these circumstances into unwanted matrimony is a New York nightmare the likes of which no one in Chicago ever alludes. We pursue the issue one step further: "Suppose they didn't make you. Would you marry her anyhow?" The response is a derisive, "Nah!" But then we want to know whether he would support the baby, and to this the answer is a subculturally typical yes. Even if, in order to do so, he would have to quit school (and our respondent values school)? Yes, even so, although, "That would be pretty bad."

The qualitative difference we wish to point up is more than a matter of nuance. Lloyd Warner and his associates were able to rank people, whom they interviewed in Yankee City, by class-typed responses to interview questions.[2] We in turn can situate boys and girls (and could do "blind," that is, without any accompanying data) in one of three impoverished subcultures, by their responses to a variety of straightforward, nondirective, and projective questions.

---

[2] W. Lloyd Warner and Paul S. Lunt, *Social Life of a Modern Community* (New Haven: Yale University Press, 1941).

Thus, a New York boy who presents a tougher "front" than the one just quoted above is still unmistakably a New York, and not a Chicago or Washington boy:

> [Do you try to avoid getting a girl pregnant or don't you care?]
> I try to avoid it.
> [Suppose you did, and she found out where you lived?]
> I'd have to marry the broad.
> [Would you like that?]
> No, that's a hell of a mess.

The less insociant type, a boy, for instance, whose presentation of self is somewhat gentler, simply says of the hypothetical girl he has impregnated: "You've got to marry her," leaving implicit why you've got to.

Since precautions to avert childbirth are unpopular, and pregnancy takes place willy-nilly, abortions should be common. If so, boys in Chicago tend to feel that it is no business of theirs. How different is the attitude that emerges in New York where, to select one of many examples, an advanced adolescent remarks apropos of a girlfriend who might get pregnant that, "If I liked the girl enough I would marry her, or something." Suppose he didn't like her all that much, would he still feel obligated? "Yeah." In what way, we wonder. Would he arrange for an abortion? "No. That would mess her up too much . . . Cause some ladies, they just do it to get money out of it; they don't really do it to help a person at all.

Nonmedical abortionists, charging about eighty dollars a job, are said to abound on the street. Nevertheless, boys recoil from availing themselves of these services, obviously not for financial reasons, which are important in Chicago, since the stated alternative, assuming marital or nonmarital responsibility for support, would be so much costlier than disposition of an undesired fetus.

The differential warmth, involvement, and concern for "the other" in sexual affairs, while significant, should not be exaggerated. It is nonetheless present whatever tack we take. The myth of *machismo*, incorporating an alleged need for constant dramatic assertions of masculinity, notwithstanding, our Puerto Rican teenage boys do not preen themselves on their virility. Most of them accept the code which prohibits tattling "to other guys about girls they have schemed with." Some do engage in invidious talk about "street girls" whose well-known promiscuity makes it impossible to take pride in having "scored" with them. Similarly, the reaction to betrayal is a mild one. Violent assault on a girl may occur if she is suspected of having squealed to the police about stealing or fighting. No so about sexual defections. When they occur, New York boys say, "I walk away," "I tell her not to do that again," "I call it quits." The gorge does not rise very high, one's manhood is not called into question, and violence flares up but rarely. Likewise, the readiness to spare a girlfriend undue embarrassment — or to share it with her by prematurely shouldering the parental responsibility — is very exceptional. Commenting on the large number of unmarried girls with babies that boys refuse to support, a respondent explains, "Maybe one guy has her, then another, and then another. She doesn't know who the father is." Then what? "The last guy gets the blame." And getting the blame more often than not seems to mean accepting the blame, which in turn (age permitting) means marriage. In this realm, as elsewhere, *fatalismo* apparently counts for more than *machismo.*

Sexual experience, which begins early and mounts in frequency if not intensity, should not be equated with sexual sophistication. Indeed, the manifest naivete is sometimes monumental. So:

[How do you avoid getting girls pregnant?]
(Long pause) I don't really know.
[Nobody ever told you about that?]
Nobody ever told me.
[Well, how do you keep the girl from having a baby?]
I guess you kill the baby.
[Do you know about killing babies?]
I don't know how, but . . .
[Is that what they do around the block?]
If they gonna kill the babies, they gonna kill theirself.
[So you never heard about protection? Like a rubber?]
What did you say? Girdle? Maybe that's the only way. I know a girl lives in my neighborhood. She had a baby, but you couldn't tell, and after awhile they found out she had a girdle on. But she still had a baby. I don't really know how you could stop it. The only way, I suppose, is wearing a girdle.

Another boy reports making a girl pregnant, but there was no baby, "Because she took it out." How, he does not know or will not say. Yet another, asked what he would do if he got his girl-friend pregnant, replies, "There's nothing I could do," and for lack of options, lets it go at that.

Early marriage ensues, in a spirit best described as resignation. This "solution" becomes all the more irrational whenever boys protest, as they do with great vehemence, that it is the one thing they wish above all to avoid. They speak of no marriage or late marriage, drawing the lesson of delay and circumvention from their own experience in unsatisfactory family relations. And, pointing to others all around them, they declaim against too many people marrying too soon, having too many children. It is on this basis that they diagnose most of their own trouble and most of the ills that others encounter in a slum environment. It all starts, they say, when a young man fathers a child he does not want — whose conception he will do nothing to prevent. Here, indeed, for one part of the underclass is the way of all flesh: fully aware of the danger, our young man tumbles headlong into it, doing exactly what he had sworn not to do, classically entering a scene he had resolved to sidestep, with some, no doubt unconscious, propulsion into a trap he professes to abhor.

A finer distinction must be made among Appalachians in Chicago. There, group-affiliated males show a consistent unwillingness to marry, holding out for very long, while among the unaffiliated there is a noticeably higher incidence of early marriage. When it takes place, males tend to be several years older than females, even if both are still in their teens. In the majority of cases, delay is secured through reinforcement of a powerful male peer group that seemingly functions much like the one analyzed by William Foote Whyte in *Street Corner Society*.[3] It is the opinion of two long-time resident observers in Chicago that "Most of the males find it impossible to maintain regular and satisfying experiences with a girl and quickly withdraw their attention and return to the male peer group." They also indicate that despite a well-nigh universal claim

---

[3]William Foote Whyte, *Street Corner Society* (Chicago: University of Chicago Press, 1955).

to early sexual experience, many of the male youths admit to prolonged periods of disengagement both from overt heterosexual activity and coed sociability. Much of the sexual play that does take place involves a group of boys who exploit one or two females, many of them "young runaways" or disillusioned young wives, viewed as "easy scores" for all. After a week or so of intensified sexuality with one such female, she usually disappears. Then the males resume their involuntary celibacy. Later they embark once again on the same cycle. All of this is absolutely affectless.

Girls in Chicago stress early marriage as a female adjustment. They hope for husbands who "won't be unfaithful," "won't drink," "will be nice," and "will work hard." Demographic findings and intimate observation make it clear that a girl, personal preference apart, often marries the first young male adult with whom she has a steady relationship. Our resident observers also tell us that their "noncodified observations yield another interesting pattern of marital relationship in the next older group," which they feel may have a bearing on "the essentially brittle relations of the teenagers." During our study, a number of marriages have been observed to dissolve into a peculiar pattern of realignments, such that: Male A, aged thirty five, establishes a liaison with Female X, his own age or older; wife of A establishes a liaison with unmarried Male B, aged twenty-five or thirty or with a formerly married male, aged twenty-five to thirty who in turn has separated from his younger wife. Consequently, for the second marriage, or for sexual adventures after a first marriage, the male is ordinarily younger than the female. We find, in short, that parallel to the traditional form (older husband, younger wife) there is a deviant form that leaves separated, divorced, and unfaithful women with younger husbands and lovers. There is a certain distinctiveness in this duality.

Fighting 6

An air of violence charges and supercharges all three of our study blocks — each in its own way. The "way" is special; the violence is not. Everyone in America is heir to a "lawless" frontier where muscle served merely as the most innocuous weapon wherewith to inflict pain on others. From the earliest Colonial period to the present moment, Americans have been almost continuously at war. With evermore destructive arsenals at their disposal, they and their antagonists contribute to the possibility of thermonuclear annihilation. Interpersonal violence in ethnic ghettos, so shocking to middle-class sensibilities, should be viewed against this background. By comparison with organized international violence, it is a barely perceptible ripple on the wave of brutality that threatens to engulf mankind. Reputable people ride the crest of that wave while the disreputable poor are somewhere deep in its trough. They experience physical assault as an omnipresent threat which, at every hour of the day, lurks on every slum corner, inside and outside every dwelling. Husbands and wives, siblings, gang boys, aggrieved lovers, cops and robbers, adolescent girls, small children, drug users and abusers, insiders and outsiders unremittingly have at each other. It is important to know what fighting means in this arena, but only if we are not blinded to the larger and bloodier arena. The subject is personal aggression and retail injury, not the far more fateful impersonal aggression and wholesale injury that constitute a real and present danger to human survival.

Asked why he fights, a Chicago boy gropes toward an answer: "I fight, sometimes when I know I can't win . . . I fight . . . I just fight to — fight!" Most respondents are more prudent: they avoid any battle in which the odds are unfavorable — for example, when clearly outnumbered and poorly armed — if it is at all possible to do so without losing face. In New York and Washington, they clobber each other, friend and foe alike. Ethnic animosity is subdued. For example, there are only residues of the old Italian–Puerto Rican rivalry, and a fading memory of the rumbles to which it once led on Manhattan's East Side. With lower class white Southern youth relocated in Chicago, the case is different. For them, racism is perfectly "natural." That they should make specific targets of American Indians and "Japs," residing on their street, and "Greeks," Puerto Ricans, and "niggers" nearby, should not be surprising. Their Indian neighbors are sometimes hunted as if they were still nomadic redskins on the wild Western plains, to be shot and killed like deer and bison. We know one homicidal adult who boasts of having murdered several Indians but who has yet to be arrested for these acts of bravado. There is a deep sense of aggrievement among poverty-stricken Appalachian whites in Chicago; many of them feel that they are being put down and persecuted as ignorant hillbillies. Their resentment does not mitigate — it probably enhances — the hostility they direct toward other "minority groups." And that hostility expresses itself in traditional forms. Sand balls, with which boys fight back home, are unsuitable in the big Northern city. Guns fit better, and, like knives, they are eminently portable.

The well-armed and aggressive adolescent boy strikes terror in everyone. Some define the fright that he inspires as "respect," and no clear line can be drawn between these reactions:

> Joe's supposed to be a gorilla, you know, a bad hustler. Everybody's scared of him. He do get a lot of respect. He got shot a couple times. Figures he's a big gorilla. They respect him too much. They think he'll kill them or something.

But, goaded by Joe, our informant challenged him one day to

"throw his hands up" and fight man-to-man. Whereupon the bully was easily bested: "Joe, he quick with the knife and gun, but when it come hand-to-hand, there ain't that much to him."

Chicagoans identify those they hate or dislike, as well as those who hate and dislike them, with much greater precision than New Yorkers or Washingtonians. Yet they may deny any antipathy whatsoever — while fighting brutally and often. The same boy who has just casually referred to five recent fights, also asserts: "I can't think of nobody around here that dislikes me . . . and nobody I dislike." The act of aggression need not be an act of hostility. Similarly, and most often in Washington, individuals may be separated from what they say and do:

> [Who do you dislike most in the world?]
> Nobody. I done told you that!
> [Those boys who curse and all. Don't you dislike them?]
> I don't dislike 'em. I just don't like their ways.

Chicago boys are least inhibited about recounting violence within the family. One recalls that three days before Christmas, he and his several siblings and his mother had a drinking party which started festively enough but deteriorated into a yelling, pushing, fighting free-for-all:

> Daddy didn't get drunk that night. He wasn't going to do it. Somebody had to stay sober. So he stayed sober, and we got drunk, and then he went and whupped us, and put us all to bed. Smacked us good, you know.

As for the mother, "He [Daddy] held her down. She was gettin' up and goin' to get her knife and kill him when he went to bed." Such scenes of domestic felicity, when not directly described, are touched tangentially by males in Chicago who, for all their family solidarity, are more willing than other boys to admit that they hate their parents.

Rage is the dominant personality trait in all three of our milieux; that quality may be turned inward or outward, supressed or externalized; in the Eastern cities, it tends to be displaced, or buried in the unconscious. Not so in Chicago where the rage is freely articulated and "acted out" with a good deal of savagery:

> This kid, he said his cigarette lighter was missing one day from the restaurant I go to, the pizzeria. He claimed I stole his lighter. So I went and told him, I said, "I wouldn't steal your lighter, man." He said something like, "Yeah, yeah." So we started fighting then. And I don't ever run from a fight. But he didn't even hit me, not once. I hit him a couple times, and he fell on the ground. Then it was all over with because after he was on the ground, I put the shoe to him. And then his eye came open where my horseshoe must have cut him or something. His eye was all bleeding. So I *really* hit him in that eye with my lighter. You know, I put the lighter in my hand and hit him. I always use something in my hand because it makes the hand tighter.

Out of the same setting comes another high school student who at first claims that he has been in trouble only for "sassing a teacher," but who, upon reflection remembers one other contretemps, "Busting a kid's head open with an iron bar." What happened?

> Well, he was a patrol boy and he started pushin' me, and I told him to leave me alone. He wouldn't do it. He kept pushin' me, and that's when I was on crutches, and I said, "Listen, you better get out of here and leave me alone." He said, "I'm the patrol boy around here, and you don't tell me what to do." So I picked me up a bar, throwed down my crutch, and busted his head open.

This jungle is full of hunters and their prey. Furthermore, all objects — including people — are potential weapons, as we see in this narrative:

> I almost got cut up here the other day. Two Puerto Ricans was walking through. They pulled out knives and they was both comin' at me, and Don — he's a big fat guy, you know — he stepped in front of me. I just pushed him on down and knocked one of them over with him. Caught him right through here, buddy. And then I got away. He's all that saved me. Big old fat guy.

Are such fights serious? Is anyone out to kill? Respondent professes to be unsure about his attackers, but knows his own motivation, quietly explaining that he "tries to kill them." In such primal conflict, things and people are equivalent:

> They use clubs and knives or anything they can get their hands on. And if they're not so big I let them pick something up. If they're bigger than me I don't even give 'em a chance to do that. When they start pushing me, I don't give 'em a chance to pick up nothin' and I don't give 'em a chance to draw back their fist. Nearest thing to me is what I hit 'em with. That big fat guy was the nearest thing to me. I just give him one big push.

The matter-of-fact attitude Appalachian youth show in interethnic violence is matched when they "fight their own kind," slashing, stomping, disfiguring, and shooting white Southern boys as freely as others. Occasionally, a felonious confederate may have to be whipped:

> One time, I went and broke into a washing machine, or, you know, me and Ken did. Actually, all I did was watch for him. I was supposed to get half the money. Well, he went and broke it, and he said, "Why should I give you money? You ain't done nothin!" I said, "Buddy, I'm gettin' that money. I'm gonna take it if you don't give it to me." He wouldn't give it to me. So I got him down hard, and took every bit of it.

The prevailing code requires that you never walk away from a fight whose preliminaries are governed by an elaborately plotted choreography. You do not provoke the fight; against all reason, you are trapped into it. Beyond a given point, not to fight is to be chicken, and there is no talking or finessing your way out. Honor calls for a duel with friend, foe, or stranger:

> Last January I got in a fight with another hillbilly. I was just standing at my locker, putting things in. He comes along, and hits the locker door and it hits me. So I grabbed him, and I said, "Say you're sorry," and he wouldn't do it. And he said he's seen me around the school. He kept pushing me, and he said, "You think you're big because you got big friends," and stuff like that. I told him, "I might be small but I'm big enough to take you without my friends." So he said, "Let's go to the bathroom." He walked in first, and I walked in behind him, and there's two

doors, one you push this way, and one that way. As I walked in, he hit me and grabbed my jaw and kicked me. He knocked me down, and then my friend Jerry got into it and threw him against the wall, and then Pendleton helped me up. So he says I'm chicken or something like that. He says, "You gotta have your friends." That's when I knocked him down, and started kickin' him in the head . . ."

The ritual, with its own collision course leading to an inevitable point of no return, the flashpoint which ignites into violence, is set forth by a Chicago boy who looks stoically on the whole business:

> When you're walking down the hall, and somebody knocks a book out of your arms, you know you gotta fight right there — unless the guy apologizes, and nine times out of ten that's not gonna happen, because you consider, well, he's out to get me. You know you're gonna fight.

The ritualized application of a strict ethic ("Never walk away from a fight.") spells violence. Chicago boys do not admit to initiating the conflict. If they respond combatively to provocation, they believe it is solely for lack of alternatives. Refusing combat would be an act of cowardice literally beyond their ken. They therefore do not plead temporary insanity, an uncontrollable temper, rampant rage, or any equivalent thereof, as very many youngsters do in New York. Blind anger, "seeing red" in the heat of passion, and general but momentary loss of self-control are also more commonly invoked to extenuate violence in Washington. Some observers, like David Matza,[1] believe that juvenile delinquents talk this way to palliate their behavior by caricaturing the sophisticated psychiatric interpretation that filters down to them. Quite a few do, repeating to us, almost word for word, the kind of colloquy reported by Matza, but only in certain cities, and speaking as fighters, not necessarily as delinquents. No such rationale can be found in our Chicago sample — for whose members it suffices that somebody else "picked a fight," that is, made a gesture which called forth counter-gestures and an inevitable sanguinary climax.

---

[1]David Matza, *Delinquency and Drift* (New York: John Wiley and Sons, 1964), pp. 42–44.

The cool attitude extends to girls in Chicago. They show no more enthusiasm for fighting than boys (perhaps a mite less) and usually their weapons are not so lethal. But, with them as with the boys, a slight, a derogatory remark or "an act of injustice" can be righted in only one way. Even the rare female who finds fighting actively distasteful also contends that it cannot be avoided. Once the confrontation has taken place, she tells us exactly what the boys have said: "You walk away and they call you a chicken." She does not walk away. Neither does she stay to reason. Pulling, scratching, ripping, kicking, and punching more or less comprise her repertoire. It starts early, perhaps as early as the second or third grade: "Now I remember. A girl took my jump rope away, and I got mad. After school I punched her in the nose, and made her nose bleed. She had glasses on, and I told her to take 'em off, and she wouldn't do it. So I hit her anyway, and broke her glasses." Later, with dating, boys become a *casus belli.* Therefore, "Martha's my worst enemy. Bobby's going with her, and I'm jealous," a sentiment the like of which no Chicago boy will ever express in regard to girls who, as contemptible creatures, are "not worth fighting about." Otherwise, with a little transposition, statements emanating from one sex in Chicago are much like those made by the opposite sex: "And Elizabeth! She's just too bossy. She threatens to beat anyone up, you know, get a gang on them, and beat them up if they don't do what she says." Here the word "gang" is used loosely. Actual members smiting each other are small, so that "gang," when analyzed, turns out to mean only a few girls — as it usually means a few boys.

With the exception of two or three other girls in her tight little circle, an informant explains that she hates all the kids, as well as the teachers, "in her room." (In New York and Washington there would be less candor about hatred for authority figures and more physical aggression directed at them, with blows exchanged by teacher and child, followed sometimes, but whimsically, by official punishment meted out to the child.) At any rate: "It's me and Vicky against five girls." And who usually wins? "Me and Vicky." With all this, a sex difference remains: girls in Chicago, as elsewhere, are more likely than boys to resolve their conflicts through intrigue and social manipulation.

Repressed aggression, while apparent among deviant and relatively isolated individuals in New York, is most pronounced in Washington.

> [You don't get mad often?]
> No, not too often. If I do, *I can't tell if I'm mad or not.*
> [Why?]
> *Because I'm used to hiding how I feel.*

Again:

> [What do you do when you're angry?]
> I just, well, if I'm angry with somebody, like on the job, I get angry and everything, but I still act like nothing really happened . . . *I just be quiet. I don't say nothing.*

Or:

> [Do you do anything to get your anger out like bowl or play tennis or drink?]
> I just can't.
> [Don't you have to do something with it?]
> No. I don't know how I do. I guess I just sleep it off.
> [Is that the best way?]
> It will keep you from hurting people.

Such characteristic attestations of quietism, retreatism, imperturability, and passivity come not from exceptional isolates; they reflect something more like a subcultural pattern of Negro youth in Washington. This pattern is the crust that has formed on top of complex emotions whose systematic concealment from one's (Negro) self and from (white) others, has roots deep in American history. The Negro has always had to simulate feelings, particularly those that might be interpreted as hostile to the dominant white caste. Practiced long enough, the simulated feeling produces personal confusion until a Negro boy, "used to hiding" how he really feels, "can't tell" anymore if he is "mad or not." The culturally and historically-induced charade by which the white man was to be deceived, has led to utter confusion. This state of mind, along with a certain kind of impotence or paralysis of the will, is not the least conspicuous mark of oppression borne by a large proportion of American Negroes. Thus, when an interviewee asserts that sleeping off his anger will keep him from hurting people, he also means that it will keep them from hurting him.

None of this is to say that Negro youth are incapable of physical aggression, but only that many more of them than whites in their age bracket are bottled-up. The same containment of emotions that makes a significant number passive now, may soon make them all the more explosive. A delinquent, describing himself as someone who has "grown into the habit of just destroying," was by his own account a nonfighter for very long, and then a very reluctant fighter. At first he allowed himself to be bullied, "to be pushed around," to be struck and provoked without retaliating. The more he shrank from his tormentors, the worse it got: "And then I realized the longer I took it, the longer it would go on," and further, more philosophically, "A person can only take so much punishment, you know, being beaten and pushed around, but sooner or later, in some way, he'll have to break out and take up for himself." At that point, the pendulum can, and in this case, did swing from apparent intimidation, unruffled and irrational calm, to absolute rage, which when it finally reached the boiling point, resulted in senseless destruction.

Whereas the collective foray is a rarity in Washington (even more so than in New York and Chicago) the fight between individual disputants, the flareup occasioned by petty disagreement, is constant. Much of this friction centers around a highly competitive and fluid rank-order, hierarchically distributed among the young. Athletic, sexual, and even sartorial competition can trigger a fight in which the victor gains at least temporary esteem among his peers. Girls, especially, are said by boys to admire the good fighter and to be responsible for many fights, an opinion offered with overtones of disparagement and resentment. We are told that fights frequently erupt at parties when boys, who may be intoxicated, vie for a girl's favor. (The situation is unthinkable in Chicago and unlikely in New York.) A teenage boy states that at parties, ". . . Mostly they fight over girls. It's really the girls who start fights at parties." Asked to be concrete, he recalls, "Well, this girl, she was talking to this one boy and her boyfriend was there, and he didn't like it. So a fight started. They argued a little while, and then they started fighting." He feels strongly that in this kind of fracas, the girls are blameworthy and the boys are not. Girls also are berated for their childishness. They are accused, in effect, of cherishing false values, actually looking up to "fellows who are tough," while professing to admire "gentlemen":

> Like I say, most of them are immature and everything. Instead of wanting somebody that's going to take them places, sort of like a gentleman boy, a boy that he come to see them dressed nicely and everything, they rather have a boy who likes to steal . . . They just want a boy that every other boy supposed to be scared of.

Battling successfully over a girl, or fighting simply, if resentfully, to win her admiration, may or may not cause his stock to rise with the opposite sex. However, it will almost certainly reinforce his self-esteem and his social standing in a community where fisticuffs, well mastered, is a vehicle for elevation into manhood. He who is reputed to be a good fighter need not fight very many times. It is only necessary to prove himself a few times for word of his prowess to spread. Nothing more clearly indicates how largely this kind of fighting is in the nature of a *rite de passage.*

It is also a species of sport, a competitive contest, an exciting game with no terrible shame attached to losing, so long as one has fought in earnest: "I ain't . . . You know, I can't beat a lot of big dudes, but I fight 'em back. That's why, don't nobody never say nothin' to me." Regardless of the outcome, initiation by ordeal takes place, and then: "Don't nobody around here mess with me." All the same, it is better to win than to lose, and best to win against heavy odds, with cleverness and resourcefulness:

> You see, I had my tennis shoes on, and other shoes in my hand. He [a bigger boy] wanted me to drop my shoes so I could fight him. I didn't want to fight. So I said, "Go away, boy, leave me alone. I don't want to fight you for nothing." But he kept telling me to drop my brogues. Then he turned around and looked the other way and I stole him [hit him when he wasn't looking] in the eye, and I almost knocked his eyeball out. He stayed unconscious for five minutes.
> [He stayed what?]

Unconscious. I knocked him cold. I felt proud of myself. I even bragged about it.

To lose under adverse conditions is not to lose all. Hopelessly outnumbered or really put upon by several others, a boy cannot be expected to come out on top. However, he can feel some sense of pride in a retrospective view of the incident:

> Somebody tried to take my coat . . . He thought . . . him and his little gang walking down the street, said, "We want your coat 'cause it's better than ours." So I told them they weren't getting it. So we just had a fight . . . All them boys jumped on me. I didn't have no way of winning that fight.
> [Did they take your coat?]
> They cut it all up, but they didn't take it. It was all cut up and raggedy when I was finished.

The responses are mixed, but a clear majority believes that good fighting makes for popularity. It serves to identify "the really tough guy" who has impressed others with his physical prowess, a quality which he can parlay into peer-group power. The truly successful bully gains a reputation that stays the aggressive hands of his age-mates. By being known as an effective fighter he may never again have to be any kind of fighter — in a subculture that severely dishonors those who refuse combat while applauding and supporting those who stand their ground. Withal, the attitude toward fighting in Washington is similar to one found widely toward stealing, namely that "It's kid's stuff." You must prove yourself as a young adolescent, and then prove yourself again only if you now seek admission to a new social circle:

> Oh, when I was small, I found myself fighting a lot, mostly with my best friend for the simple reason that he could always find the worst thing in the world to irritate me. But as I've grown older . . . well, only one fight sticks in my mind, and that was after I first moved out of the area that we were talking about. I was playing football with some fellas, and . . . uh . . . I guess they were trying to find out what kind of a fella I was. In my opinion, it wasn't necessary to show this fella that I wasn't afraid of him, but I did, and I didn't do too bad at it either . . .

It is, then, a bit burdensome and wearisome to have to reestablish what should have been clear long before, through all the early years of brawling every day or every other day or "about twice a week." Advanced adolescence, properly traversed over many prone bodies, brings with it the right not to fight. Power becomes something Robert Biersdedt maintains it always is, namely *latent* force, a mere potentiality that nevertheless causes people to do what you want them to do.[2] Power also consists in self-determination; a "rep" frees one to do much on his own that might otherwise meet with resistance: "People aren't going to mess with you . . . If you go someplace they'll know you. If you're a good fighter, your name spreads." From this standpoint, name and fame are a passport to freedom, at least freedom from constant molestation. Not that approval will ever be universal. Adults may disesteem you for exactly those traits that yield status and power to you among your peers:

> Street fighting don't make you popular with the neighbors, or anyway with the older stage of people in my neighborhood. They don't like it. But in the younger stage they do. Most of *them* are out anyway to get what they can get, and beat anyone that they can beat . . .

But the pressure to fight, even if it displeases elders, is overwhelming:

> See, I was scared that if I didn't defend myself, they'd come after me, and find out where I live, and that one day they'll be waitin' for me, and when I come outside, they'll be ready to jump me. So I figured I might as well fight and get it over with.

Neither does ascendancy as a fighter necessarily relieve you of all further need for battling. At least one Washington skeptic thinks it is risky, "Because if you get to be a good fighter, then some other boy is going to come out from Southeast or Northwest and want to take you on, and you find yourself with a busted jaw or something like that." Those fists which have won peace within the

[2] Robert Biersdedt, "An Analysis of Social Power," *American Sociological Review, XV*, No. 6 (1950), pp. 730–738.

community, at least for their possessor, may act as a magnet, drawing challengers to oneself from outside the community.

Even though success in one's face-to-face society may be paved with good aggressions, Washington is less fearsomely and violently hostile within its own confines than any other area we have studied. And only in Washington do we once or twice hear the defiant voice of reason, for instance from a youth whose motto is "Let's talk it out."

> That's the first thing — talk it out. If it can't be talked out, then deal with it in other ways or try to work something out. I try hard. I don't like fighting too much because if you fight, somebody's going to get hurt. Then you both might get hurt bad enough to go to the hospital at the same time. I try to avoid it.

In East Harlem, parents beat their children, rarely suspecting that there is any other mode of discipline. Once in awhile, the children strike back directly; more often they displace the aggression onto peers or comparatively vulnerable authority figures. Brother strikes brother and sister strikes sister. Yet the family is an immensely cohesive unit. Nothing so surely precipitates a fight as a real or fancied insult reflecting on any member of the family:

> So then, you know, I hit this guy in the face. My cousin kept hitting him in the stomach where he finally stabbed him. Then my mother called us and said, "Leave that poor boy alone."

But why all this? Because, "He said my grandfather is dead, he's a bum, he's not going to heaven, he's going to hell."

On the inviolability of their families, New York girls talk very much like New York boys, and act accordingly:

> Just a few nights ago, this man pulled a knife on my father. Now, I'm a very patient person. When I was a kid there used to be a boy who kicked me, literally, in my behind every day, and I never bothered with him. But when you get to my family, all my patience is gone. Look out for blood . . .

Reasons for the omnipresent threat of assault are exceedingly complex; more depth psychology than we had at our disposal would be required to probe the matter; but most of it, as put to us by Puerto Rican respondents, is clearly triggered in the family milieu. In a number of cases, one part of the cycle starts with an injury inflicted on a sibling — followed by an injury inflicted on oneself:

> [Were you ever so sore that you went into your room and knocked the wall with your fist?]
> Yeah.
> [Over what?]
> Over when my brother wouldn't let me do nothing. That makes me mad. I get mad at him, and I fight him, and when I lose, I sock the wall.

Repressed wrath, so pronounced in Washington, so nearly non-existent in Chicago, is a distinctly minor reality in New York but it is there. Sacred vis-à-vis outsiders, parents and siblings may be struck. Such action, however, serves to increase, not to relieve, tension. In that eventuality one of two outlets is available: self-flagellation, which rarely occurs, and wanton aggression on the street, to which a larger proportion resort. Much the same sequence of affect leading to action moves and mobilizes either sex. A girl feels most enraged when Mother screams at her: "That really makes me mad, but I don't say nothing. Like, if I say something to somebody, I'll jump on him. I just want to fight." Or Little Brother wants help with his homework: "And I say, 'You can't learn it by *my* doing it.' And he starts yelling at me, and I get mad, and throw his books at him." Then Big Sister unnerves her: "I had a blouse on. She wanted to wear it, and I had already washed and ironed it. I threw a shoe at her. She went and told Mother." With all these irritations accumulating in the close quarters of tenement life, our girl bursts out onto the street, where other girls, also seething, are happy to engage her in combat.

A slur on one's mother, specifically the term "motherfucker," can be enormously provocative unless delivered in a jocular vein or modified and used adjectivally as an all-purpose word: "The only time you catch me fighting, you have to curse my mother . . ." Or, "On my block, you curse anybody's mother, you know, and they knock you out." A boy observes:

> I don't hardly get mad.

[What *does* get you mad? If somebody calls your mother a name, what do you do?]
One day, when I was in school, this guy show me a picture. He says, "That's your mother there." I almost stopped him from believing he could breathe any more by holding his breath. Used a karate motion I learned from a book.
[On karate, in passing: "I learn some ways to hit, how to kill. I learn how to kill somebody. But I don't try. I try to break a jaw. I hit him over here, and I kill him. I learn that by myself."]

An exceptionally pugnacious girl whose diminutive stature is a source of misery to her, for she believes that it provokes classmates into taunting her, fights when she is "called a bum for fooling around with the boys." She confesses, as hardly anyone else does, to "looking for trouble" that will eventuate in maximum use of fists and nails on taller girls, a pastime which she professes to enjoy: "When I'm in the mood, it's fun." For all her personal idiosyncrasies, she reveals the family context within which this pleasurable aggression takes place. Asked, after she has boasted of several victories, whether she wins all her fights, the girl replies:

Not sometimes. Sometimes I lose, and I don't care. And sometimes I cry because I'm too nervous. Some of the girls go home for their mothers, and I start running for my home. So then, my sister Lucy, she comes out and starts cursing at the girl's or boy's mother. And there's a lot of fights with my sister. She thinks she's tough, and she's always looking to beat me.

And so on — into the more predictable familial tack.

By sharp contrast with youth in Chicago, and markedly moreso than in Washington, New York boys and girls take "uncontrollable temper" to be an essential part of their psychic makeup. Fits of violence are ascribed to this temper, which is hypostasized as a thing apart, entering the individual and controlling him as if by diabolical possession.

This little guy I know, when he get mad, he take out a knife and he want to stab you or something. Once this big guy named Jorge, you know him, he was hitting the little guy because he wanted to throw him off the street. He said, "Get out of here," and the little guy wouldn't. So he slapped the little guy who got real mad, and he picked up a pipe, and hit, hit here [motioning]. He broke the pipe on him. They had to send that big guy to the hospital for three weeks. When he get mad, he get like crazy . . .

With *lex talionis* at home, in regard to older and stronger adults (for it is hardly ever considered correct or possible in New York to hit a biological parent, although stepfathers are fair game), violence explodes in other directions. One teenager lets it be known that whenever he yields to a temper tantrum, it is necessary for him to break things. "Things" on one occasion boiled down to "cement in my bathroom." What made him so mad? "Well, I wanted to go downstairs and my mother wouldn't let me, and I started saying I want to go down, and she hit me, and . . ." We may speculate that as the Negro child deflects violence from untouchable whites, so the Puerto Rican child sometimes refrains from raining blows on the head of a parent he is supposed to revere. In either case, children punish themselves for acts they have not committed — with the difference that a normative pattern in Chicago is a deviant pattern in New York. It may also occur in Chicago, but there we almost certainly have no pattern at all. The range, then, would be from expected to peculiar to downright abberant behavior.

The young Puerto Rican who is goaded by intolerable frustration into "breaking things" is but a step away from breaking heads. Among the available heads are those of pupils and teachers. Consequently (but not only for that reason) the schoolroom and environs become an additional center, providing many more opportunities for physical conflict, offering substitute targets for those that are disallowed. In school, youngsters react with great sensitivity — as if their skin had suddenly turned inordinately thin — to the arbitrary exercise of authority. They do not deem such authority to be as legitimate as that of parents, even when parents protest that it is. A boy, describing one of his friends:

He don't like nobody to push him. And when it's time to get out of there [the school], he can't get out. The teacher push him, and he take out a knife to stab the teacher. And everybody have to hold him. He get like crazy, and then the cops come.

They take him to his house. His father ask him, "How come you get mad like that?"

Another boy who thinks that the worst thing he ever did was to hit a teacher in the face, explains that he had no right to perpetrate so serious an offense. He judges it to be serious because, "That's what my mother says." Does he agree with his mother? "Yes, indeed." Well, we wonder, would he do it again? "Yes." And then in an effort to reconcile these contradictions, he disposes of the problem as follows: "Yeah, it's wrong, but if the teacher bothers you, you got a right to hit her." The badly thwarted schoolboy has a low threshold of tolerance for anything he construes to be obnoxious, offensive, or bothersome in teachers. One further example:

> [Did a teacher ever hit you?]
> Oh, yeah, a teacher, he pushed me.
> [Why did he do that?]
> He thought it was me that was throwing stuff around . . . He took me by the shirt and he pushed me. I pushed him back, and he took me downstairs . . . So, I had to send for my mother.

The school is also a major locus of combat in Chicago. There, however, no one in our sample reports aggressive attacks on teachers; person-to-person conflict means pupil-to-pupil conflict. Violence is accepted, and projected in the dominant imagery, as a permanent part of social life. Boys expect regular threats to their status and to their manliness which can be resolved only by violence, and thereby, the continuous reestablishment of personal identity:

> [So every day there's always a chance of getting into a fight. Something's always happening?]
> Yeah.
> [Why do you think this should be so?]
> I don't know. It never bothered me.
> [Every day there's the possibility of a fight. Doesn't it disrupt the whole school system and your whole way of life?]
> No, I don't think so.
> [Do you get what I mean?]
> No, I don't think so.

In answer to the question whether fights are between friends or enemies, a Chicago boy says: "Well, between enemies. And when the enemies get done fighting, they're friends." Fighting to heal a breach is considered indispensable for the comaraderie that it engenders. Violence is felt to be functional (as Lewis Coser and other Mertonian sociologists say)[3] if for no other reason than to prevent even greater violence. A girl speaks out of her long experience as an observer of street and school fights:

> Whenever there's a fight between two persons, and they have personal reasons for fighting, nobody should stop them from going ahead and finishing the fight. Otherwise, they'll just get a gang together, and finish the fight that way. But they want to settle it right then and there by themselves. Once it's settled, it's all over with, and they're friends. But, if they get started and they get broken up somehow, they just want to fight all the time. Let 'em finish it the first time, and that's all you're going to hear out of 'em.

Conforming to school rules is a problem for many teenagers, producing an upsurge of anger directed not at adults who make the rules but at other boys and girls, like yard marshals and crossing guards, who attempt to enforce them. During early adolescence, Chicago boys find that their fights take place almost always in and around the school where there is a confluence of youngsters with whom they cannot frictionlessly agree on norms that are worked out in residential areas. The sanctity of social space comes into play as they grapple with each other over boundary maintenance mechanisms.

Out on the street in New York, even now, despite a widely reported decline in bopping behavior, there are still gangs abroad, and with them, the danger of "being jumped" by marauders equipped with zip guns, 22's, bottles, rocks, knives, and baseball bats. Of these sanguinary clashes, their temporary cessation and periodic resumption, we have a quantity of narrative accounts. The eclipse of large-scale gang warfare is popularly attributed in

---

[3] Lewis A. Coser, The *Functions of Social Conflict* (New York: Free Press of Glencoe, 1956).

New York to the advent of drugs. Yet, the same eclipse is palpable in Washington and Chicago where the use of drugs is relatively inconsequential. In each city echoes of an old situation can still be heard. Older boys refer to the social block as their "turf" or "territory," but they do not nowadays have "negotiations," or "truces," and "treaties" with formally organized street-corner boys in adjoining neighborhoods. War counselors, clubhouses, dues, arsenals, and official position all belong to another era. A club jacket is the contemporary insignia. Club members do join together for offensive actions, but at present they are uncommon occurrences.

From depredations and altercations of every kind, whether as victim or aggressor, and from the more ferocious household squabbles, a small number of boys and girls totally withdraw. They are often the psychopathically passive and technically nondelinquent youth. Whether they are "healthier" or more "normal" than the psychopathically active and technically delinquent youth is a moot question. On the face of it, and with some supporting evidence from projective tests, we are ready to hypothesize that some of them are among the sickest children in America. If so, then violence in and of itself, is a poor index to social pathology.

Stealing 7

When a teenager flatly asserts that, "Everyone on my block steals," he is overstating the case which must be hedged and qualified, but not by very much. Nearly every youngster on the slum block, whether in New York, Washington, or Chicago (with few but conspicuous exceptions) does develop some kind of "larceny sense." In all probability, while still quite young, he will learn to steal and he will learn what the risks are — including when, where, and how not to go too far. Just as experimentation with sex approaches universality, so with theft. For the maladroit, the unlucky, the less intelligent, and the more masochistic, disaster may follow, but those who greatly (that is, officially and institutionally) suffer from it are never very numerous.

The impulse to appropriate things is identical in all three cities; similar factors heighten or dampen it; but specific urgencies and opportunities are palpably at work in each case. Thus, many boys of every class are booked in the United States for car theft. No offense is commoner or more likely to result in detection. Even police records in a given locality sometimes (as in Detroit) reveal a higher incidence of car theft among middle-class than lower class boys. Most of them, whether privileged or underprivileged, are apparently more interested in the "kicks" that accompany a joyride than in taking possession of someone else's property. Chicago boys are different: They want cars and car parts, sometimes to sell, but most often for their own use. For white Appalachian adolescents in Chicago, the car is an extension of the self, an almost organic appendage without which they are less than whole. In this respect, these youth are more "Americanized" or "middle-classified" than the most slum children. They inhabit the world of Marshall McLuhan in which technology intimately impinges on and integrates itself with the individual. The world of Timothy Leary is much more significant to New York boys who are surrounded by a drug culture that is rivaled in pervasiveness only by certain psychedelic communities in California. Washington, lacking any such *Weltanschauung*, still has its peculiarities. Notable among these is dog theft and the dog lore that goes with it to guarantee proficiency and profits. The knowledge is transmissible; one individual learns it from another, but then typically he goes out alone to commit the act:

> Most of the time I go out by myself. See, I like dogs, German Shepherds, Dobers. I got a Dober now about this tall [motions], see. If I spot one out there I want I think I can get, I try for it the next night or something.
> [Do you sell it in the neighborhood?]
> No. That's taking a chance of getting popped. I take them to ——— Circle where all those white people are. See, they love these German Shepherds and Great Danes and Dobers, and you can sell them for a good price. Or you can take them out to ——— Street where all those farmers come in at. They like dogs too. I sell a Dober for $80. See, these people who have papers on them, when they sell them to the public, they sell for $200 or $225 and on like that. A Dober has a nastier background than a Shepherd. He'll turn on you, you see. You can trust a Shepherd better than you can a Dober. These people, they love vicious dogs.

Chicago boys like to stay in motion. It is their motif. Small children who steal toys prefer model cars and airplanes, graduating at a later age to full-sized vehicles or anything detachable that may be on and in them. For intermediates, there are bicycles and motorcycles. Not just stealth, but tricks of the trade and mechanical skills must be developed to a fairly high degree. Finally, a Chicago boy is able to differentiate automotive parts as knowledgeably as a New York boy can specify the various kicks that accompany different drugs. Each learns early in life something equivalent to the dog-fancier's expertise in distinguishing between breeds and their market value. Dogs, drug habits, and cars: all require special care and feeding. Cars run out of gas, and gas is expensive: "The tank was almost empty. We had to get gas somewhere, and we didn't have any money. So we found another car, and stood there and siphoned it out." Cars are stripped, with speed and precision, on the street and in back alleys. Boys rebuild their own cars, carefully selecting parts they need or parts that are in demand, sometimes selling their loot at junkyards whose receivers of stolen goods ask no questions. Much of this is utilitarian, but some of it is esthetic. Bikes and cars have accessories, adornments, status symbols, the addition of which will arouse envy in other guys. And they have their effect on girls who are believed to admire "sharp" car thieves and to enjoy, as an especially piquant experience, riding in stolen cars and motorcycles.

Car ownership is beyond the ken of adolescent boys in New York and Washington. Like middle-class boys, they therefore steal cars only for joyrides. Both the joy and the ride are very brief: they may not last more than a few blocks. And yet our interviews turned up no instances of a car stolen for any other purpose. The culprits are invariably located by the police in short order. Momentary use and not sale is the purpose. Girls who go along on these short sprints, not necessarily knowing (and always professing not to know) that the car is "hot," may wind up in jail:

> I was in a stolen car once . . . We were sitting there, and the boy said it was his father's, and we said, "All right." So he was going to take us downtown somewhere. We got up to ——— Street and ——— Avenue and I got frightened because he said it was a stolen car, and I jumped out. My girl friend, she got caught, but I ran away . . .

The serious thief in New York is most likely to be a drug addict. Driven by an inexorable compulsion to acquire cash with which to buy heroin, he views cars more realistically: "You swipe the car easy. But it's no good to swipe because they always catch you." The technique is explained by another addict–informant: "There's a couple ways. You get silver foil. On the old cars, like on the Mercurys and Fords, there's three screws, and they're shaped like this (shows us). So, in between them screws there, you put the silver foil and it makes contact. It starts. You can start it from the engine too. I use the silver foil underneath. It's the easiest for me because I can put it in and take it out when I want to." Not that he wants to — for only the parts are marketable: "Now let's suppose you swipe the wheels and you swipe the radio and you swipe the motor and the batteries and all of that. You can get rid of it. You can sell it. But you swipe a whole car, how can you sell a whole car?" The supply of parts is unlimited, the demand constant and usually specific:

> You go around and hear them talking that they need a wheel, they need a battery, and they only got so much money to give you. So you take a guy aside and tell him you could get it. If you don't know the guy you tell him, "Give me the dough, and I'll bring you the wheel. You keep the dough and don't bring him no wheel . . . If I know you and you need a wheel, you tell me the size and stuff, I go around walking normal like, and I look at all the wheels and I figure out which one you need. Then I go get the rest of the guys, and they haul up the car while I pick up the wheels, and we take that one wheel.

Our informant and his companions have proceeded countless times in this way; none of them has ever been arrested; but he reports a close brush with the law: "Once this cop car came down, and everybody split. They caught me because nobody told me they was coming and I was taking off the wheel. But as soon as they put me in the car, I jumped out and made my cut . . . It's easy to slip away." Bad luck dogs another addict who says, "Yeah, I even get away and I still get caught. How do you like that?" The addict seeking wherewithal for his next fix and the boy who wants a brief joyride look to cars. In New York and in Washington, they are a small minority. In Chicago, cars overshadow everything else. They are as crucial to the dominant life style as camels are to Bedouins or snow is to Eskimos. In all cases a special technical language is richly elaborated around their principal preoccupation. Here are excerpts from the small talk of a self-taught Chicago expert who knows all about cars, not least how to steal them without getting caught:

> We call Earl's car The Missile. It's big, it's long, it's fast. Rat's is the Cheese Box. I call mine the Blue Angel because it's blue and when it gets goin' it flies. Yours [to interviewer] would be a Tomato Can . . . I'm just glad them quads didn't kick in . . . You can get a car that's got a deuce on it. You can get deuces or quads or a four barrel. That'll make it faster . . . A deuce is just one carburetor with two holes in it for gas to come out of. Three deuces is three of them with two carburetors. I got a manifold at home like that with three carburetors. When you pull your gas pedal, all three of 'em open up. That's why I told you I wanted to get a coupe, one of them little flatheads . . . A quad's just one big four barrel. Two quads on one manifold. And that's eight barrels kickin' in instead of four. Of course, quads might tear the transmission up if it's automatic. Only a stick will ever hold up to it. Then you can set your linkages on the floor, get four-speed, everything. And man, you can speed shift, just hit the clutch twice, keep the gas down, and toe it, and it's gone. That's all.

Petty shoplifting is universal. Sooner or later every respondent in all three cities admits to it. A sophisticated, college-bound teenage New York girl is certainly simplistic in her analysis of stealing, but in referring to herself and her peers, she touches upon a small part of the truth:

> Most of them steal because they don't have clothes to wear, you know, decent clothing. They rob a pocketbook, and then they'll go out and buy some shoes, maybe for their little brothers and sisters. To me this is not wrong. Listen, basically I'm not a stupid person. I have stolen things in my life.

If we are to believe her, she stole clothes only for her younger siblings — rather often, and like so many others, without being apprehended. (The extent to which upper-middle-class youngsters in suburbia "boost" clothes, a phenomenon which of late has led to considerable public alarm, would of course serve to refute the implication that poverty *causes* shoplifting.)

Other less altruistic teenagers and preteenagers concentrate on stealing clothes for themselves, with hardly any sense that it is "wrong" to do so: "Like some guys, they go in the clothes department and rob a couple of pants, some shirts, socks, and shoes. That's not so bad." This respondent is hard put to say what *is* bad, but after some silence and much prodding, he does offer two examples, namely, "Robbing blind people and taking money from collection boxes in church." To take off directly with clothing from a store or, out of greater desperation and more bravado, from a dwelling, and to rob to get money to convert into wearing apparel is important among our East Harlem and Washington youth. Says a New York boy, who could as well be speaking for those like him in Washington and Chicago, "Sometimes we develop another kick, stealing from taxis." He expounds the technique, the timing, the use of decoys, the excitement and then the pleasure that follows this and other kinds of stealing, and, above all, the opportunity "to go buy some clothes." (Again, this advanced adolescent who became a virtuoso of sorts, robbing and stealing "most every weekend," like his brothers and friends who taught him when he was "twelve, thirteen years old," never got caught.)

Empty homes and apartments in the neighborhood, nearby shops, and midtown or downtown department stores are prime targets. Slum dwellings obviously do not afford lucrative possibilities and they are often avoided for that reason. Yet you can never be quite sure: "When we went in somebody's empty apartment, we found boxing gloves, we found wine, we found bicycles, we found golf balls."

The "we" is vital, for most of this thievery is, from first to last, a small-group affair. We find occasional lone wolves in New York and Washington such as the boy who claims always to have gone on clothes-stealing expeditions by himself: "I used to put things on and leave my old clothes there." But, as Austin Porterfield[1] and other criminologists have pointed out, the lone wolf moves under

[1] Austin Porterfield, *Youth in Trouble* (Fort Worth, Texas: The Leo Potishman Foundation, 1946).

exactly those conditions of exposure most conducive to arrest and further entanglement with the law. Repeated arrest means incarceration and differential association with more experienced thieves. Speaking of a loner: "No, I didn't went with him. Anyhow, he used to get caught. So he don't go no more [to a large department store]."

The totally alienated addict also operates on his own, putting himself in greater legal jeopardy by stealing for sale than by buying and ingesting drugs — a violation for which policemen claim that it is hard to secure evidence. To our question, where does he steal, an addict answers in effect, anywhere and everywhere, and literally from anyone — with an alleged second thought, however, about those closest to him, like his mother. Strolling through stores by himself, he would, "Grab anything, and make it and run." He finds easy pickings at every point. Along any street there are cars from which various objects can be removed. Breaking into apartments that are preferably but not necessarily unoccupied, offers more possibilities. In a way, even as a last resort, "Mother's place" is the easiest. From it one may abscond with: "Like some records. She had a whole bunch of them, you know. So she wouldn't find out, I would take half of them. Something like that it would take her a long time to suspect." The daily need for money may not be excessive ("I try to go for only enough for me to get high. That's all . . ."), but it is an incessant and often an increasing need that will almost always propel a monomaniacal addict on his own into direct confrontation with the law.

In the economically impoverished areas of New York and Chicago and in much of Washington, all such single-handed predatory crime is peripheral; some kind of collective behavior, involving at least one other person, is central. The boy who is queasy about stealing frequently will have his masculinity called into question, and fighting to prove otherwise cannot be counted on to resolve the question. Thus, most explicitly, "I tell them, 'I'm a man. You know, don't call me a sissy. Don't bug me.' We start a fight over that." Later on the same boy says with unusual frankness, "When I go stealing, I got to be with somebody because I get scared being by myself." Or, a teenage girl, looking back to her habitually lawbreaking past: "I was always invited. I never went on my own. I didn't care for it. I never stole anything. I just used to be the lookout. I'm too nervous." Nevertheless, when out helping to steal, she did it, in her words, "Mostly every day," and has not entirely ceased to do it, although so far — that is, for a period of some years — the police have not molested her. She protests that stealing really goes against her grain. Originally, "I didn't want nothing to do with it," but for this the other girls stigmatized her as "chicken." Yielding to social pressure, "I was stupid enough to join them. I should have said, 'All right. I'm chicken because I don't want to do what you're doing.' I didn't think twice. I just went right on ahead and done it."

Washington youth tend to make stealing, like fighting, a somewhat more individualistic process. Whereas shoplifting elsewhere is for the most part a group activity in which young adolescents indulge more than their juniors or elders, no such chronological progression exists on our Washington Street. The national pattern includes a "tapering off" at approximately sixteen which is not discernible among Washington youth who continue to shoplift at more or less the same heavy rate in all age categories. When this behavior is devalued by the peer group in one community, generally as "kid's stuff," it gains no further support, and participation markedly declines. Where the lone operative is at work, presumably actuated more by his own anxiety than by group pressure, larcenous acts appear to continue beyond any special age limit. A gang may generate reluctant or enthusiastic stealing, which eventually ceases to be a focal concern of the group. Sanctions are actually imposed by the gangs on those who perseverate in a manner deemed appropriate only for boys and girls who are expected to outgrow their childishness. The overage, late-adolescent shoplifter invites scorn, and he loses his companions in theft, he too is likely to cease and desist. The individual shoplifter, who never belonged to a gang, feels no such collective constraint. He is less likely to give up his pilfering. Unchecked by significant others, this kind of delinquency is bound to last longer.

We recognize that ostensibly individual motivation also has social sources, but they are not necessarily the same as those which evolve in highly stylized and ritualized group activity. Lone wolf stealing à la Washington, may be embedded in the larger social structure which richly rewards the self-reliant individual. In New York or

Chicago, to steal successfully, with frequency and finesse, ordinarily enhances one's reputation within a clique, a gang, a small group of peers. Overtones of admiration and respect are plentiful as one Chicago girl describes another: "She got a pair of shoes, a skirt, a shoulder bag, black tights. That girl, she can just walk in a store and pick up anything." Or: "She'd take wallets or something . . . and go to the cash register. You know, they'd open the cash register and turn around to ask someone if he needed help. She'd just reach down in there and get the money out of it . . ." And again, speaking of friends, presumably more venturesome than the respondent, we learn that, "they see something they like, maybe a necklace or some expensive thing, and pick it up and walk out with it." Ineptitude is a major deterrent to shoplifting. So we ask, "If you could do it without getting caught, would that make you popular?" and the answer is an unqualified, "Yes!" But, in Washington, the successful thief who is less dependent on a few age-mates, does seek honor in the larger community. His exhibitionistic display of booty is intended to accomplish that end. He splurges freely, wears new and expensive clothes, generally practicing conspicuous consumption to make it obvious that he has many things others around him cannot afford. Two quotations, among very many, express this sentiment (which participant observation strongly confirms):

> They steal because they want to say that they got plenty of money and brag about how much they got — something like that. And get themselves nice things.

More to the point:

> Younger boys will look up to an older person like that [one who steals]. They'll spot him and say, "I know that guy," and they'll say, "That man knows enough. He can really steal." It makes them look up to him. I don't know why. But sometimes you hear them say, "I hope I can steal like him when I get big" — or something like that.

The more or less organized collective exclusion (or personal and individual withdrawal and recoil) from stealing turns so often on questions of competence and aptitude that boys rarely take girls along on their two-, three-, or four-person raids. It is often said of girls in New York and Chicago — mostly by boys but also by other girls who take this sex difference for granted — that, "They talk too much," "Sometimes they squeal," "They're clumsy," and that reprisals against them result in unnecessary complications:

> If you go with a girl, and you get in trouble, she say you took her stealing, and then you gotta beat her up, and that get you into more trouble.

Much better not to take her along. Nevertheless, here and there we come upon a girl who transcends the reputation for weakness and unreliability from which her sex suffers (by these adolescent peer group standards.) Hence, this disclosure from an exceptionally bright and articulate young lady in East Harlem who seems to be accepted as one of the boys:

> I've been with the guys who go crib bustin' — you know, house stealing. I stay in the hallway or downstairs. Since I'm good at whistling, they usually take me. I stand downstairs, and they can hear me all the way on the top floor whistling. They never got busted when they was with me, and I never got busted. I know things. If I was to be taken into a precinct, and you know, be interrogated, they'd tell me, "Well, we want you to tell us this and that." If I was to open my mouth, a lot of people on our street would be in jail, even the people that were decent. I like my skin, and I don't want to shed it . . .

An older girl will sometimes steal for (but not with) her boyfriend, helping him even if it means wronging a parent:

> I didn't want the money for me. See, I was going out with this guy Johnny at this time, and he had bought a car. His boss had gave him eighty dollars, and he needed twenty more because the car was $125 or $150. I don't remember. And I knew this guy who he had bought it from, and he told me that if Johnny didn't give him the twenty dollars by that night, he was going to take the car back, and I wanted Johnny to have the car . . . So, I went to my mother, and I was going to try to get five out of her, and all of a sudden a twenty dollar bill popped out of her purse. So I just took it and walked out.

Minutes later, she exclaims: "You wouldn't catch me robbin' no Gimbel's," an enterprise best left to boys who "are better at it" and have "more experience." As for herself, "I don't think I'm fast enough, you know."

None of this is to suggest any greater moral delicacy on the part of girls than boys. Another New York girl who insists that she "never touches anything" in stores, reveals fewer qualms (than we have learned to expect on her street) in taking advantage of small children, conduct which even the average gang boy will shrink from. Her story follows:

> There's this little boy who'd just run away from a home about three weeks ago. Out of pure dear meanness he snatched this lady's pocketbook. I mean, he had money on him; he didn't need it. Somebody must have dared him, or he was just mad or something. I really don't know why he done it, but he went and snatched that pocketbook. She had just collected her number. She hit her number, and she went to collect her money, and when she came back, on her way out, the little boy probably found out. So he snatched her pocketbook and ran away with her money. Two hundred and thirty dollars. I got ten of those dollars 'cause I found out that he stole the money. I told him, "If you don't give me ten, I'll take all of it off you." You know, he's so small. I got me the ten dollars.

The chance factor is enormous: slight complicity in a prankish offense can produce big trouble; regular systematic stealing may have no untoward consequences. Apart from numerous life-histories, we would offer as indicative, if less than evidential testimony, an impression that emerges in this recurrent type of exchange between interviewer and interviewee:

> [Tell me, who do you think does more stealing, boys who have records in the court or boys who do not? What's your opinion?]
> The boys who don't have records.
> [Why do you say that?]
> Because I know a lot of them.
> [Why is it that they don't have records?]
> They're smart, that's why.

Or: "There are a lot of guys that don't do too much, and they get caught. Maybe it's the first time they went into a certain place, they only got bad luck." Among those who are brought to book for their infractions, contingency is king. Every official, like practically every youngster, is aware of this truism. They know that some serious offenses are lightly punished and that some minor offenses are severely punished. National figures show that girls undergo institutionalization as delinquents at a very high rate for alleged incorrigibility or unmanageability. These rubrics generally signify sexual delinquency, and the complainants are usually mothers. Of late, people who go by the public record report more girl truants and runaways, also sought by mothers who cooperate with the court in sending their wayward offspring to correctional establishments. In the summer of 1966, New York City Police declared that, for the first time, they knew of more missing girls than boys. Disappearing for short intervals and spending a few days with grandparents, aunts, or friends is a phenomenon common to young people of both sexes on all three of our study blocks. It arouses more maternal concern in the cases of girls than boys. For their protection, the police are more likely to be notified, and the wheels of justice more rapidly set in motion. In Chicago, one girl, speaking of a friend, says: "She kept on skipping school. Miss N. [her aunt and guardian] found out about it, and talked to her, and sent her off to Montefiore for three years." Another girl in the same group tells us, however, that, "When you ditch school, they don't say nothing to you . . . You don't have to bring a note . . . Teacher don't say nothing." School officials do not figure prominently in this drama; parents and parent-substitutes do. Hardly anything but a parental summons brings the unhappy girl into contact with police. A pervasively hostile and contemptuous attitude toward the female on the part of Appalachian whites would certainly account in part for the frequency with which Chicago girls "get into trouble." An informant explains that this trouble is usually a product of, "Running away from home, and trying to elope or something like that." "Girls," she goes on, "try to get away from home because they don't care anything about their parents, and they think their parents don't care anything about them. They just want to get out, and they run away." Then what happens?

Sometimes they go over to their girlfriend's house, you know, and spend two or three nights there, and then go out running around the street and go over to their boyfriend's house maybe. If they have enough money, they get them an apartment. And policemen are usually looking for them. So they have to stay in all the time.

Staying in all the time means staying away from school. Thereupon, a vicious circle sets in, from mutual rejection in the family setting through "running around the street" and loose sexual behavior to voluntary or involuntary truancy: "No, they can't go to school because the police are looking for them there too." A high probability of arrest and incarceration goes with these circumstances; our Chicago interviews are studded with opposite examples:

. . . Jane was sent away to Audy Home for running away. She'd just leave her mother and father. They'd catch her and put her in Audy Home.

. . . Annie's been sent to Audy Home once or twice for leaving home. And, if she gets one bad thing, like someone telling or lying on her, they'll believe it, and she'll be back in Audy Home for two or three years.

And so it goes in a customary pattern that also involves leniency toward girls who "take things" as most of them do, either for excitement or for other reasons.

Very little of this larcenous behavior is grandiose or seriously criminalistic, although, to be sure, that little includes some well-protected affiliation with the organized underworld. A relatively few boys, whose names may never appear on a police blotter, become runners in the numbers racket or low-level pushers in the narcotics trade. These boys, whom we directly encountered in New York, are headed for criminal careers under optimal conditions for their safety, if not society's. They are as statistically abnormal as are those at the opposite extreme who never steal at all. In between lies the great mass, steadily stealing away. Whether "cool" or perfervid, their behavior can only impress the observer by its extraordinary pettiness. As reported to us, good "loot" for an average group of teenage thieves in New York is $10 to $15 —

which, when evenly divided, comes to about $3 to $5 for each culprit. What to do with such sums of money? "Drink, buy something to eat. If you have a girlfriend, take her out to the show on Sunday. Blow pot, sniff glue, play cards, gamble." Since these pleasures are mostly reserved for weekends, a marked increase of petty theft occurs (most noticeably in New York, a little less so in the other cities) on Fridays and Saturdays:

> I don't steal on the week, only on Saturday.
> [Saturday is stealing day?]
> Yeah.
> [Does everybody steal on Saturday?]
> Yeah, we get together. Then we go to separate stores. Whoever don't come up with something is a chump.

"Yoke robbery" is the Washington name for a serious variant which is no specialty of any one group. These are the remarks of one Washington boy:

> Two summers ago, I guess I was too young to be employed, but I didn't have a job and didn't have any way of getting money, and a couple of boys with me, they were both in the same situation. So, every Friday night we would go out together, every Friday night, to try and get some money. That was like mostly everybody I knew.

A group of boys would disperse, small clusters of them moving out in different directions, all bent on yoke robbery, for whose nature we were offered the following explanation:

> Well, we go in front of a beer joint or somewhere like that, usually a lively beer joint with a lot of people in it. When one of the men come out intoxicated, we grab him and take his money.

Although he knows others who have sometimes been arrested for this weekly activity, the police have so far failed to interfere with him. Still, this kind of robbery is rough and dangerous. A yoke job is best executed with three boys, one to grab the victim if he struggles, one to hit him and another to go through his pockets, "all at the same time, all in one motion." Noting that wallets and keys are seldom returned, our informant adds: "One time we yoked a policeman and threw his badge in the mailbox."

> [How did you yoke the policeman?]
> Same way we do anybody else . . . He tried to struggle back and everything. We hit him a couple times. He broke loose; we kicked him; he fell down. Then we went into his pockets, hit him again, pushed him into an alley, and ran. I think he got up, but we had gone by then. Caught the bus.

Boys and girls steal clothes simply to wear them, or, along with other "hot goods," to sell them. And selling is no problem. Markets differ in each community, depending on what people prize at any given time: conversion into cash is exclusive of professional "fences" who play no part in these transactions. Each market is as large as the neighborhood in which it is located, encompassing all those who want to buy cheap. Ten shirts may be "snitched" from a haberdashery and sold at a dollar each. A specialist in good transistor radios is able to dispose of them for ten dollars each. (He and his friends in New York like to swipe radios from homes. We wondered how frequently this sort of thing takes place. Answer: "Let's say if we know there's an empty apartment right now, we go over right now." Well on in their teens, unaffected by the general preference for Saturday stealing, none of them has ever been in the toils of the law.)

Another question put to another New York youth: "Do you guys have regular customers?" "No, not really, but a lot of Spanish people, if they know you have something good, they say, 'Come here, let me see, let me see it.' I mean, if you sell it clean, they'll buy it." On further questioning, we learn of one whose needs are well known and easily met. Specific demand for other items is not uncommon: "Well, there was this construction up on ——— Street, and we stole some wrenches and stuff like that. We sold them all brand new, and since he [the purchaser] works with plumbing, he bought them . . . For a nineteen-inch wrench he gave us three dollars, and then we had a ten-inch wrench, and when he gave us a dollar for that, we just left."

A high school boy who says that he "used to steal a lot" and who apparently loses no opportunity to do so now, reports his most recent theft, "Last Saturday I stole me a pizza . . . I say, 'Gimme a pizza,' and then when the man puts it down, I take it and run . . . He said, 'Get that kid.' It was too noisy, so nobody heard him. Then I hid in the building, and he went by. He forgot all about the store. Then he run back." The same day, this boy stole several pairs of nylon stockings, making sure to pick the right size for his girlfriend. Stolen goods do not enter his home: "My mother asks too many questions." This kind of stealing in candy stores and discount shops is endemic in and near each block. In many cases, there, or farther afield, the risk appears to be incommensurate with the gain, which is almost always negligible. Here, however, one should not overlook the element of play. Whatever else it does, outwitting a subway guard or outrunning a pizza proprietor provides fun and excitement.

At first we were puzzled by the frequency with which children (particularly those in New York) told us that they stole "only little things." Could this mean that the misappropriation of "big things" seemed more criminalistic or more offensive to the moral sense? A better explanation came so persistently from our interviewees that it could not be ignored:

> I used to take candy, never big things.
> [Why not big things?]
> Because if they catch you stealing little things, they don't do nothing. They only tell you to get out of there.

> I only take small things. Pies or cakes.
> [Is it wrong to steal big things?]
> Yeah.
> [It's right to steal small things?]
> No, it's wrong. Both of them are wrong.
> [Then why don't you steal big things?]
> Because I don't want to. You might get caught too easy.

And:

> I used to go stealing with my friend, but I didn't pay attention to him. So, if they catch him, they don't catch me . . . He stole stuff like gloves, put them in his pocket . . . Once he got caught.
> [What happened?]

They took him to a back room, and they left him there, and they called his mother, and his mother took him home and gave him a beating.
[How often did you used to go stealing?]
Around every day.
[Why didn't you steal yourself?]
Because I was older than him.
[You mean, if you got caught, you would have been in big trouble?]
Yeah.

Not moral revulsion, then, but a prudent calculation inhibits many young people from committing offenses which they otherwise countenance. "No, I was never afraid of getting arrested. I just figure it's not right," comes from a rare soul responding to the dictates of conscience. For most of the rest there is no "inner check," no deeply internalized value system or superego. Therefore, they steal when and where it is safest to do so, taking those things that invite minimal penalties. After a certain age, wherever the authorities draw their legal line, those penalties go up — and the petty larceny goes down. Everywhere we see a certain amount of rational caution, but no moral fervor. The dominant attitude cuts across crimes against the person as well as crimes against property:

[Is it considered bad to take a girl and rape her?]
Oh, I don't do that.
[Why not?]
I don't want . . . they give you a lot of time for that — if you're caught.

Juveniles who are arrested and hauled before a judge realize that they are being subjected to a good deal of unpleasantness, but they do not fully anticipate the serious consequences in store for them. Claude Brown, author of *Manchild in the Promised Land,* testified before a Congressional Committee (as reported in the *Washington Post,* August 30, 1966). His statement certainly applies to dark-skinned slum dwellers, if not to the whites in Chicago:

You're going to have a police record if you're raised in a ghetto and you can't get a job with a record. You can't even work for the poverty program because if you're got a record they can't hire you.

Brown urged that "felony sheets" be wiped clean. He recommended passage of a law making it impossible for a man to be denied work in Federal, state, or local government because of a criminal record. The record includes arrest with or without subsequent conviction and whether or not the person is technically a juvenile. Private employers, as well as government at every level, simply exclude a large part of the most needful population from respectable employment by automatically rejecting anyone who has ever been arrested.

Such are some of the long-range effects a youngster is rarely able to perceive. They will be understood when it is too late to undo what the law has done. Ironically enough, that law — in fact, the whole apparatus of juvenile treatment — was contrived to protest minors from being stigmatized and punished before they had attained their majority. Below a fixed and arbitrary age, children were not to be defined as "responsible" offenders. Theoretically, they are still irresponsible; actually, their accountability extends even to arrest, and much depends on arrest alone. Since none of this is understood by the young slum child, he does not fear it. With his orientation to the present (a quality often ascribed to the poor which, however, Kenneth Keniston has found to be characteristic of alienated upperclass boys at Harvard University),[2] he fears only restriction of freedom, confinement to an institution, obvious and drastic punishment in the here and now.

A New York boy remarks about juveniles who "get busted" that, "They're stupid. They do stupid things. They don't watch what they're doing or nothing. The other guys, they're slick and they watch what they do. Before they take something, they look around to see if somebody's coming." Minors who do get caught are well aware that nothing worse will happen the first time or the first few times than that they will be sent to a children's court and will be put on probation. The fortuitousness of arrest or non-

---

[2]Kenneth Keniston, *The Uncommitted* (New York: Basic Books, 1965).

arrest, with all that follows for one's life chances, can scarcely be exaggerated:

> [What happened when you got caught stealing the car?]
> They let me go.
> [For that they let you go?]
> For that they let me go. The guy didn't want to press charges, that's why.

To the extent that criminal law is not administered in a wholly capricious manner, it reflects certain age and sex expectations in American society. "Boys will be boys" and they may violate legal norms whose transgression by girls would provoke the public to cries of moral outrage. And vice versa. Similarly, actions regarded as deviant in adults may be tolerated in minors — or vice versa. These differentiations are crystalized in contacts with the law, they are bruited about and their meaning is absorbed in slum communities: "One day I got caught housebreaking with two other guys. They said I was too young. If I was about sixteen years old, I would be locked up. But I say I was fifteen. So they just called it delinquency." Boys who prankishly stole $22 in school from their teacher, although threatened with severe reprisals, made partial restitution, and no action was taken against them. They continue to perform delinquent acts — with impunity — inside and outside the school area.

On the basis of our own findings we would warmly endorse the observation made by two sociologists, John F. Clark and Edward W. Haurek:[3]

> Official statistics are indices of negative *social response* (defined as the reporting and handling of misconduct) to behavior and not necessarily indices of the actual quality and quantity of juvenile behavior although the two phenomena may be highly related.

And further, as these authors cautiously put the matter:

---

[3]John P. Clark and Edward W. Haurek, "Age and Sex Roles of Adolescents and Their Involvement in Misconduct: A Reappraisal," *Sociology and Social Research, I* (July 1966), p. 496.

The results of "admitted delinquency" studies would appear to meet some of the objections to the use of official data. Although this research technique has its limitations, it does provide data that are relatively free from the distortions imposed not only by the nature of the operations of formal social control agencies but also by the informal structures that intervene between the misconduct of juveniles and their referral to these agencies.

All "admitted delinquency" studies, including our own, establish the virtual universality of juvenile "misconduct." Realistic fear and increasing maturity militate against continued misconduct. For this reason, today's delinquent is rarely tomorrow's professional offender. To persist in the petty larceny of one's early years is to be guilty of inappropriate role behavior, to be involved beyond one's years in "kid's stuff." The vast majority of admittedly delinquent young people settle down, marry, go to work, eschew criminal careers, and no more (nor less) seriously violate laws than most of the rest of us. Since our laws go far to guarantee that lower class "junkies" will become adult offenders, drug addiction knocks this pattern into a cocked hat. All available evidence on institutionalization indicates that many, but certainly not all, hardened graduates of training schools also take the criminal path. Yet another decisive factor must be considered, namely, employment. Settling down, which presumes a job with steady wages, cannot be taken for granted when a high proportion of slum-bred youngsters are unemployable. To be out of school and out of work is, at this writing, more than twice as likely for Negro as for white youth. Job discrimination, which bears heavily on all minority groups, hurts young Negroes most of all. The job door will more often close to nonwhites than to lighter-skinned Puerto Ricans, and more often to them than to white Appalachians. These irrationalities cannot be ignored. They are stitched into the fabric of our society. To look closely and steadily at that society is to see that our so-called culture of poverty is less important than the poverty of our culture.

The extent to which that larger culture, "American culture," has significance for poverty youth is our next concern. That a "culture of poverty" is multidimensional across poverty groups and determinative of highly variable behavior patterns seems reasonable to conclude. Nevertheless, establishing the presence of material deviance (stealing) — whatever its variability — might lead us to believe that certain elements of "materialism," a cultural value of the larger society, has filtered down to the occupants of the underclass and has provided the essential impetus toward delinquent behavior. It is, at least, the general formulation widely, though not universally, shared by sociologists of the contemporary American scene. Yet, as we shall offer, this explanation of delinquency has been more conjecture than fact, particularly the notion that the ideology of success in the material world takes its place as a moral priority among all Americans, regardless of social class and cultural (or subcultural) persuasion.

8 Levels of Aspiration and the Ideology of Success

How deeply embedded in the very nature of man is his commitment to illusion and aspiration? For Thomas Hobbes, in *Leviathan*, all men, though unequal in natural endowment and learning, were equal in hope. In his view, man, at once a rapacious and reflective creature, relinquishes his natural biological appetite and enters into some form of social order in which imagined states of grace are attainable. Once a social contract has been established, the human being moves from a purely antisocial animal existence and becomes a social organism, exchanging his destructive natural impulses for constructive accomplishments that are generated by his hope.

In any society, whether primitive or advanced, some measure of symbolic futurism is built into its institutions. No natural desire ever exceeds mankind's imaginative calculations. As in the Freudian formulation, the pleasure principle reaches its completion in the shape of an illusion. Man, as a *social* being, rarely exceeds in his imagination those elements of hopefulness which are defined by his cultural and social experience. Hope is never unlimited, and we are tied to the boundaries established for us by the society in which we individually develop. So, for example, even those regarded as deeply disturbed in their mental processes draw heavily, if not entirely, on the cultural forms available to their experience, no matter how unusual their illusions. However, part of the measure of social change for any group is its capacity to push slightly beyond traditional prospects, extending the level of hope for that group a bit beyond its previous level of enterprise.

In the broad historical picture, hope takes two essential directions. In one, there is the prophetic promise of millennial redemption; man, unable to improve his condition in this world, attains it instead in a symbolic afterlife. Although no society totally relinquishes its millennial hopes, their prominence as supernatural conceptions remains a premodern phenomenon.

In the second direction, men gravitate toward hope rooted in the here-and-now, exploring the secular prospects of individual and social advancement. The industrial revolution, in particular, encouraged visions of the good life on earth (though these, of course, were amply evidenced from the beginning of time). Where preoccupation with the external hereafter has not simply vanished, it has ceased to be regarded as a suitable orientation toward the future, even among contemporary religionists. Mechanically transformed, immersed in the technical processes of his environment, twentieth-century man has set his sights on those means by which a better existence is obtainable within his own life span.

In American society, the rapid pace of economic and technological change has developed within the framework of an equalitarian social and political ideology. This system, under law, ostensibly affords the same opportunity to every citizen to attain the better life for himself by effort and initiative. Thus, the most popular culture hero frequently reenacts a version of the Horatio Alger theme. "Rags to riches" is consequently a staple of national imagery. Indeed, so widely has the idealization of equal opportunity and unfettered aspiration been disseminated through our mythology, that it has come to be *assumed as an unquestioned fact of American cultural and social life.*

Anomie and Opportunity

In the past few decades, sociologists have focused their attention on the significance of this ideal. They have used the "drive to success" as a significant variable in attempting to explain many endemic social problems. Two major avenues of inquiry have been pursued. We have had studies designed to examine the structural limitations of opportunity in American society. In general, they show that opportunities are severely restricted in a rather rigid class system. These studies leave no doubt that achievement possibilities are most imperfect though the society proclaims its egalitarian intentions. The excellent empirical work of Robert and Helen M. Lynd,[1] Lloyd Warner,[2] and John Dollard[3] made all this clear long ago. More recently, continued discrimination against minority groups has dramatized the degree to which segments of this society are denied access to the "open" system of opportunity.

An intersecting line of sociological inquiry has sifted the empirical evidence to buttress a theoretical explanation which holds that many types of social deviance result from the *unfulfilled, ungratified hope for material success* among underprivileged classes of people to whom the usual avenues of advancement remain closed.

Beginning with the incisively logical and now classical essay by Robert K. Merton, "Social Structure and Anomie,"[4] many sociologists in the United States have contended that there is a commonly held, society-wide level of aspiration, but that the lower strata, blocked from attaining that level, include significant numbers of people who have recourse to "innovation," that is, to crime and delinquency. No theoretical formulation has had greater impact on the work of sociologists than Merton's essay which, through successive refinements, has produced many hypotheses about the disjuncture between aspirations and opportunity and how it leads to a condition of "anomie" in modern society.

Anomie, a term introduced by Emile Durkheim to describe a state of "normlessness" in some societies,[5] presumably arises when man's hopes and aspirations exceed his ability to fulfill them.

---

[1] Robert S. and Helen M. Lynd, *Middletown in Transition* (New York: Harcourt, Brace, 1937).

[2] W. Lloyd Warner and Paul S. Lunt, *Social Life of a Modern Community* (New Haven: Yale University Press, 1941).

[3] John Dollard, *Caste and Class in a Southern Town* (New York: Harper, 1937).

[4] Robert K. Merton, "Social Structure and Anomie," reprinted in *Social Theory and Social Structure*, rev. ed., (New York: Free Press of Glencoe, 1957) pp. 161–194.

[5] Emile Durkheim, *Suicide* (New York: Free Press of Glencoe, 1951).

Individuals, striving for the unobtainable, are deprived of normative restraints and controls; hence, they engage in innovative, illegitimate activities. Their purpose is to overcome the obstacles which confront them and to do so by any and all available means. Where a society offers culturally acceptable goals but fails to provide legitimate means adequate to their attainment, the structural condition of that society is, perforce, anomic.

For Merton, the situation is described as follows:

> A high frequency of deviant behavior is not generated merely by lack of opportunity or by this exaggerated pecuniary emphasis. A comparatively rigidified class structure, a caste order, may limit opportunities far beyond the point which obtains in American society today. It is only when a system of cultural values extols, virtually above all else, certain *common* success-goals *for the population at large* while the social structure rigorously restricts or completely closes access to approved modes of reaching these goals *for a considerable part of the same population,* that deviant behavior ensues on a large scale.[6]
>
> . . . When we consider the full configuration — poverty, limited opportunity and the assignment of culture goals — there appears some basis for explaining the higher correlation between poverty and crime in our society than in others where rigidified class structure is coupled with *differential class symbols of success.*[7]

Merton, and other social scientists following his lead, have compiled an impressive array of arguments, all set forth with admirable rigor, suggesting that deviance is a natural byproduct of social pressures impinging upon the lower classes of American society.

At the core of this analysis, however, is an *assumption* that the value of success is a goal shared at some point by virtually all members of this society, no matter where they are located in the continuum of social stratification. Yet, despite the fact that some degree of rigidity in the class system (especially at its base and at its apex) has been established by empirical study, little evidence, in the form of measurable data, has been adduced to prove that success, as defined in the middle class, pervades all of American social

[6] Merton, "Social Structure and Anomie," p. 146.

[7] *Ibid.*, p. 147.

life. There appears to be a general consensus that, as compared to other socioeconomic systems, ours is relatively fluid. At the same time, it is apparent that a kind of "cultural lag" has developed, so that values clustered around the poor man's desire for upward mobility far exceed the opportunities available to satisfy them. Hence, anomie. "In this setting, a cardinal American virtue, 'ambition,' promotes a cardinal American vice, 'deviant behavior.'"[8]

"Hard" data accumulated so far have been primarily suggestive and inferential. Investigators have drawn their conclusions from widely diverse sources. Sometimes they extrapolated from census tract data, and, more recently, they have induced results from highly structured scales designed to measure anomia, the individualized effect of the social-structural pressures brought to bear on specific populations. In general, almost all the data gathered, whatever their relative degree of validity, have tended to substantiate the initial assumption that pecuniary success is a totally pervasive American value. In addition, the broad criminological picture seems to lend its statistical weight to the notion that delinquency is largely a class-bound phenomena, disproportionately concentrated in, and really a mark of, the underclass. Still, theoretical calculations have greatly outraced and outpaced actual findings; unfortunately, the theory has overshadowed the research.

Some important empirical exceptions to the alleged rule that pecuniary success is an ubiquitous American goal have only recently appeared in attempts to test the Mertonian thesis. Mizruchi in *Success and Opportunity*[9] indicates that lower-class people place greater emphasis on security than on the acquisition of wealth, a finding akin to others independently reported by Meir and Bell,[10] Hyman,[11] and Inkeles.[12] Furthermore, many of the facts that seem

---

[8] *Ibid.*, p. 146.

[9] Ephraim H. Mizruchi, *Success and Opportunity* (New York: Free Press of Glencoe, 1964).

[10] Dorothy L. Meir and Wendell Bell, "Anomia and Differential Access to the Achievement of Life Goals," *American Sociological Review*, *XXIV* (1959), pp. 189–202.

[11] Herbert Hyman, "Reflections on Reference Groups," *Public Opinion Quarterly*, *XXIV* (Fall, 1960).

[12] Alex Inkeles, "Industrial Man: The Relation of Status to Experience, Perception, and Value," *American Journal of Sociology*, *LXVI* (July, 1960).

to support Merton may only be artifacts, and the theory, with all its speculative insight, could stand or fall on those facts. So, for example, though official statistics show much higher rates of crime among members of the lower class, most criminologists would agree that these rates are biased. They are more a product of the response of control agencies than a true index of the distribution of crime and delinquency throughout the society.[13] Our own data, already presented in the chapters on delinquency patterns, tend to support this contention, at least insofar as it pertains to lower-class communities.

In the field of delinquency, an important extension of Merton's thesis was developed by Cloward and Ohlin in their influential book, *Delinquency and Opportunity.* According to these authors, a delinquent subculture will develop when legitimate means for the attainment of success goals are inaccessible: "The disparity between what lower-class youth are led to want and what is actually available to them is the source of a major problem of adjustment. Adolescents who form delinquent subcultures, we suggest, have internalized an emphasis on conventional goals, and unable to revise their aspirations downward, they experience intense frustrations; the exploration of non-conformist alternatives may be the result."[14] One alternative is the use of illegitimate means to attain conventional goals. Another involves participation in illegitimate opportunity structures. A third type of response is embodied in the retreatist gang or group, composed of those who are "double failures" — unsuccessful alike in their use of legitimate *and* illegitimate means to success (for example, drug addicts).

Moreover, in a particularly important passage bearing on their major hypothesis, Cloward and Ohlin suggest it is not necessary to show that a large proportion of persons in the lower class exhibit a high level of aspiration. Rather, ". . . it is sufficient to show that a significant number of lower-class members aspire beyond their means if it can also be demonstrated that these same persons contribute disproportionately to the ranks of delinquent subcultures."[15] And,

[13] Edwin H. Sutherland, *White Collar Crime* (New York: Dryden Press, 1949).
[14] Cloward and Ohlin, *Delinquency and Opportunity: A Theory of Delinquent Gangs* (New York: Free Press of Glencoe, 1961).
[15] *Ibid.*, p. 88.

although they offer much discussion from a variety of sources concerning their hypothesis, they adduce no new evidence with which to validate their conclusion that delinquent youth in fact are those with high aspirations who have experienced insuperable obstacles to their achievement.

This then becomes a major focus of our inquiry. We have shown that delinquency patterns vary markedly in three lower-class study areas. And so we raise the question: Are these variable patterns traceable, in any or all three of the communities, to problems stemming from unfulfilled and insatiable aspirations? On the contrary, as we will attempt to demonstrate, social and economic realism is the rule. High aspiration among the three impoverished groups of youth in our study is almost nonexistent.

The Deprivation of Imagination

In pursuing this matter, our approach remains highly qualitative. Although the total number of youth interviewed in the study areas comes to over 130 — a number more than sufficient for quantitative study — we decided to probe the full spectrum of aspirations, from lofty dreamlike ambitiousness to hard-headed realism. We asked each respondent to "let his imagination run loose" over the full range of conceivable employment, income, and residence — not just those possibly available to him, but those a fairy godfather might offer. We expected that quite a few would reach impossibly high, and then come down to earth with a thud as reality intruded on their fantasies. It is clear that, though our poverty youth may be rich in fantasy in other ways, aspirationally they are almost painfully deprived. Where these youth aspire to a fairly high level — they represent less than 25% of the total interviewed — some at least realistically recognize that they will be able to approximate their goals only if they have taken meaningful steps toward upward achievement. These youth are essentially committed to completing their educations, and — for our purposes a most critical point — they have rarely engaged in delinquent acts.

For example, a male Negro respondent in Washington states:

> Success? That's a very large word as far as I'm concerned. Well, so far, let's just say after I've gotten out of high school,

say when I got this job right here, I made a little success in attaining my goal. I have myself a good job now. I can, let's say, more or less get me anything I want because I don't have any responsibilities whatsoever. . . . I think I have been successful. I had my education paid for. All I have to do is get into college right there. I think that's on the way to success.
[What kind of work would you like to be doing the rest of your life?]
The rest of my life? Well, that's why I'm trying to go to school now — to be a student first, then a lawyer second. That's what I really want to be — a lawyer. I think I'll be a pretty darn good one . . . I know first it takes four years of college, possibly three or four years of law school — because I want at least three years of law school. And after that, I'll probably stay two or three years to try to get another degree — possibly to get a doctor's degree or something like that. I'd like to shoot as high as I can go.

Other youth with high aspirations are much less optimistic. One Chicago boy who would like to be a lawyer describes his problem:

[Why would you like to be a lawyer?]
I don't know. I guess cause they talk a lot. I fit in there perfectly.
[Do you have any idea what a lawyer does?]
Yes. I have an idea of what a lawyer does. He makes good money, I can assure you of that.
[What kind of thing does he have to do on his job?]
He . . . he either condemns 'em, or . . . In other words, helps 'em to get locked up, or maybe even sent to the death house, maybe even be the one that executes 'em. Or he could be the one that gets 'em out of an execution. But, it depends on whose side you're on, who hires you for the best price, or whatever. That's just like, say, people out here hire you for a job and they don't tell you what you're running up against. That's the same way with a lawyer. He never knows what he runs up against until he's right there.
[What kind of work do you think you'll do for the rest of your life?]

Digging ditches mostly. Probably digging ditches. Or I'll be running machines — punch press, drill press, screw machine, hand screw machine, automatic screw machine — so forth like that. I figure I'll be running these types of machines. Not too good of jobs, but jobs, you know. Enough today, at least it's a job.

In this case, the aspirational comedown is severe. Allowing his fantasy to run full range, he speculates about being an attorney and, unlike our Washington youth, he has made little effort in this direction. Yet, when he is deflated, his expectations fit those that are most frequently the currency of youth in this community — to be employed as laborers or factory workers. This pattern, as we shall see, occurs in each community studied. Occupational aspirations, though differently specified in each area, tend to be culturally patterned within each community. So, in the Chicago area, factory work is the expected occupation and one to which youngsters generally aspire; in Washington and New York, skilled and semiskilled occupations, such as those of mechanic or carpenter, are both aspired to and expected. In these instances, though high aspirations obtain, the expectation is either consistent with them or much lower, but, almost always, they remain within the framework of that which is expected and patterned by the community.

Only infrequently do we encounter pure fantasy in connection with occupational success. Here a young Washington Negro male, who otherwise wishes to be a cook, responds to our question concerning success:

[What does success mean to you?]
Success?
[Success, yes.]
Couldn't tell you.
[You have no idea?]
Wheel . . . big wheel, or come a success . . . becoming a lawyer or anything like that.
[So you think success to you is becoming a big wheel?]
Yes. I think you could be a little wheel and be successful . . . anything, anything you do. Like something you been trying to do for the last five years and you finally become successful.
[What do you mean by big wheel and little wheel?]

Well, a big wheel . . . I'll tell you, got most of the money. They got, you know . . . they can go out here and do most anything and get away with it. You know, crap games or gambling. They own these big places and stuff like that, or you know . . . And they can do almost anything, speed or anything, you know, in cars. Or they don't get no tickets, you know . . . I don't think.

The same young man, when asked what a good salary would be, states: "About $85 a week. That's a good salary for someone my age, I think." Yet he does not "know" his future salary and is unable to guess about it.

At the opposite pole from that rare individual who looks to a future in one of the professions are those in a state of occupational *atonie* — an inordinate listlessness and lifelessness — a condition more severe than mere *anomie*. From this type we can evoke no more than an unemotional "No" to our questions, "Do you want to get ahead in the world?" and "Do you have any ambitions?" And no amount of indirection, exhortation, or free association will produce anything more.

Between the extremes of realistically and unrealistically ambitious and totally unambitious youth, we find most of the others. They would like to move up a notch or two above their present station. The following are typical responses from each of the three study groups.

A Puerto Rican male youth typifies the respondents from this community:

[Do you want very much to get ahead in the world?]
Yeah.
[What do you mean by get ahead?]
Well, I'd have a good job.
[Suppose you had any one of your choice — this is heaven now — any kind of job. What would you pick?]
If I had any kind of job?
[Yes.]
I would get an office job.
[You'd like to work in an office? Doing what?]
Maybe typing or . . .

[That would be the best job you could imagine? Typing?]
No, it wouldn't be the best.
[What's the best you can imagine? Dream!]
That's kind of hard.
[Can't think of any?]
No.
[Well, what do you think you will wind up doing? In jobs? When you settle down for the rest of your life?]
Maybe something that has to do with stock work in department stores and things like that.
[How much do you think you'll earn?]
I won't make too much. Maybe about eighty or something.

Again, a Washington male youth:

[What kind of work would you like to do for the rest of your life?]
Wash dishes.
[Wash dishes in a restaurant?]
I think that's clean. More clean, like, that's clean work.
[Anything else you would like to do?]
Cook. Cooks make pretty good money.

And in Chicago, a male white youth responds to the question about his occupational hope:

A steel job like my dad is doing.
[You want to work at hard labor. Have to lift heavy things, move around?]
Yes.
[Would you rather work in an office and wear a shirt and tie?]
No.
[Why not?]
'Cause for those kind of jobs you gotta get up too early. And there's a secretary that tells you . . . sits in your lap . . . takes notes for you. I don't like them to come in and sit on my lap. I saw on TV, this was a true story and this man, he was sitting down. He had a suit on and he pushed a little button that called his secretary in. And the clothes that she wore to

> work — she didn't have on! She had her nightgown on, that you could see through it. And she came in and sat on his lap and says, "You ready?" And that man said, "I want you to take a note for me." And he kept looking all over her. And she set down on his lap and he started goofing off with her. And then she got up and slapped him and walked out.

These youth appear relatively satisfied with their moderate ambitions, willing to settle for those jobs that are realistically available to them. For most, it is impossible to elicit discontent or to inspire them to register even a modicum of frustration. They envision the occupational world within the framework of that community of occupations surrounding them — so little are they inspired by powerful success-orientation. Rather than being motivated by "relative deprivation" as Merton and his continuators maintain, they appear to settle for a social and psychological plateau, perhaps best described by the notion of "relative contentment," primarily influenced by the cultural setting of occupational possibilities present in the communities where they have been reared and socialized. Whenever those pieces of cultural success-orientation from the external world breach their enclosed community life, they are viewed as secondary possibilities and rejected for the most part as foreign matter.

Among the poverty youth studied, both social class and the neighborhood subculture are strategic influences in prevailing occupational and pecuniary success levels. More than 70% of these ethnically diverse youth, though markedly different in their delinquency-conformist patterns in each study area, share a realistic orientation toward occupational placement in the future; this rather large proportion *aspires* to a level equivalent to *expectation*. Those who wish to be carpenters expect to achieve that goal; those who want to be secretaries expect just that; those who aspire to be factory workers also expect it will come to pass. Very little discrepancy between aspirations and expectations appears. Nor do the dominant goals appear to be unrealistic.

Of course, some are undecided about occupational choice, but their indecision is more a function of their *personal* and *idiosyncratic* dispositions than any synthetic culture conflict. For them, the level of aspiration is still relatively low. For example, a girl from our New York sample states:

> I like a job where I could be on the go. Moving around, you know, doing some filing. Going from here to there. In a restaurant where you have to move with a dish here, run with a dish there. Something where I don't have to be . . . you know, where I could sit around and look at things and I won't ever get bored with it. [There was this job] where the books were about that thick. There were four books — big, gigantic. Everything I used to look at, you know . . . Like I got so used to seeing that small print that when I used to look at something, I used to see the print on people's faces, you know. Seems like everything I looked at had that small print. I got tired of it fast. Then I had to start wearing glasses and I hate them. And I quit right away.

Or, a Chicago Southern white youth who, like so many of his peers, daydreams about cars:

> I want to go around and see different parts of the United States. I don't like to stick in one place. I don't want to settle down in one place right now.
> [What kind of work would you like for the rest of your life?] It's hard to say. I wouldn't mind working . . . I don't even mind pumping gas. I like anything that has to do with a car, put it that way. I'll go sit and look at a car all day long. I'm not sure what I'll do. I may get a job and just keep it, even if I don't like it. I mean if it's easy, I'll keep it. If it isn't, then I'll find a way to get fired.

Still, some remain who are unhappy about their occupational future. They represent a very small proportion of those interviewed. To what do they attribute their discontent? Two major sources are indicated. On the one hand, the social community around them has produced almost insurmountable obstacles for attaining their goals. These youth, perceptive as they may be, stand out as a small proportion of all those who feel dissatisfied. Nevertheless, they are not pronouncedly more or less delinquent than other youth in our study. They speak with deep resignation as young people who must settle for something less than they would like. The forces of control in the social universe far exceed their capacity to manage their own objectives. This factor is decidedly more marked for girls than boys.

In New York, a Puerto Rican female youth states her dilemma:

> [Do you think there's any use struggling to get ahead in the world?]
> For a girl, no.
> [For a guy?]
> Uh-huh. Like getting a job. But sometimes I sit down and think of things. I'm going to get a high school diploma. For what? I'm going to end up getting married and getting a baby and being in a house. The high school diploma will be hanging on the wall. I ain't going to be using it.

A Puerto Rican boy points to educational deficiency as the solid rock upon which his aspirations are regularly broken. He aspires to be a lawyer. He believes his chances of succeeding are "very rare." He explains: "Because if the teacher doesn't understand me in school, they don't give you a chance to explain."

Or, as another puts it: "When you without a high school education, it's very hard." And, "That's the trouble. In school I couldn't get along. I know I couldn't get along in college. Plus I wouldn't get there."

On the other hand, the *primary* interpretation for failure to get ahead is not a perception of structural obstacles but rather a highly personal explanation. As they see it, some deficiency of their own leads them to an inevitable dead-end. A young lady in her late teens tells us:

> Well, there is one thing I always wanted to be: an airline hostess. But I'm too short. That was one thing I had put in my mind I wanted to be, until someone nice and kind had to tell me that I was too short.
> [What do you think you will do if you work?]
> Nothing. I'm too stupid and simple. I'll never get nowhere.

If there is any single ideological consensus that pervades these communities and is shared by the majority of their youth, it is not an image of pecuniary success but an interpretation of failure, whatever the level of aspiration. Paradoxically, those youth who match their aspirations with a sense of reality, and expect nothing more, see failure overwhelmingly as a function of personal inadequacy. This value not only permeates explanations of occupational failure and success, but also extends to behavior within the deviance–conformity configuration. (This will be explored more fully in Chapter 9.) It appears that they have succumbed to, or been suckered into accepting American society's smug interpretation of virtue vis-à-vis vice as a highly individualistic process: to fail is to be a victim of one's own shortcomings and not the shortcomings of the system.

This ideological expression of individual inadequacy as the basis of social placement is well documented in *Mass Persuasion* by Merton and his associates.[16]

> But to the extent to which these sentiments are echoed by those who regard themselves as "working class" or "poor class" is even more revealing. Consider, for example, an elderly housewife, with a small income and of limited grade school education, who reaffirms the legitimacy of present arrangements: "*People with good heads deserve more. If my head isn't as good as another one, why should I get the same as you?* I didn't try hard enough for it. . . . *How do people get rich? They're smarter than we are.*"
>
> A small shopkeeper, viewing herself as poised between "the rich" and "the poor," points to the essential incapacity of the poor as the chief reason for their plight: "*I imagine poor people are poor because most of them are poor managers.* People like us, we're more in the middle class. We don't see too much hardship. I'm very sympathetic to sick people, but really poor people — it's always their own fault."

From these examples and others, Merton himself demonstrates that failure to achieve high economic levels does not necessarily lead to rebellious, withdrawn, aberrant, or criminal behavior. The system is perceived as a fair one; the individual blames himself for his failure.

---

[16] Robert K. Merton, *Mass Persuasion: The Social Psychology of a War Bond Drive* (New York: Harper, 1946), pp. 168–169.

Just as occupational ambitions are modest, so are income orientations. Most youth hope to earn a "living wage" somewhere between $75 and $100 per week. The income aspirations and expectations coincide with remuneration generally available in the occupations they desire. Occasionally, they wish to make more, but rarely does that figure exceed $125 per week.

When we asked them to conjure up a windfall ("What's a lot of money?"), their responses were humble, most often involving amounts from one dollar to a few hundred. And what would they do with the money? "Buy a Coke," "have a party," "get my car worked on," "buy me some clothes," and occasionally when the fantasy burgeoned, "help my mother and put some money in the bank." In other words, do pretty much the same thing that they do now, except do it a little more.

Where do they wish to live? What is the most desired residence? Despite enormous dilapidation in each of the study areas, the sense of "staying with one's kind of people," of "being at home," of gaining pleasure from one's community of persons (rather than the physical community) far outweighs residential aspirations to move "up and out."

One youth, a respondent in our New York sample, imagined coming into a sizable fortune. He said he would like to move somewhere else, "downtown," denoting a desire to change his physical surroundings. We suggested, "Possibly Park Avenue?" (a wealthy section of New York). He responded, "No, that's too much. I would spend too much money there. I'd move down, like at First and York, to the Projects [Public Housing developments], except you can't." Here, he desires to move to a community not too far from his peers and relatives and just a cut above his present level. This same youth aspires to earn $100 per week and to be a cabinetmaker, an occupation and income he expects to achieve without too much difficulty.

Illusion Anchored in Reality

In all, our findings are relatively simple. We have recorded in-depth interviews with youth of low socioeconomic status in three ethnically diverse social communities, a matter of critical empirical significance. We observed their various levels of aspiration in occupations, money, and residence. And although each community of youth was shown to exhibit diverse patterns of delinquent behavior, they had in common one important attribute — a low level of aspiration. If maladaptation exists in these groups, we would venture to suggest that it is not a consequence of the disjunction between opportunity and an internalized value system disproportionately stressing "success." Our study populations exhibit a generally adaptive orientation to the economic world which they eventually will face — no matter how truncated this world may appear to be. A major reassessment seems, then, to be needed in the theory that economic "anomie" is the compelling determinant behind social deviance which manifests itself as delinquency among lower-class youth. Illegitimate "innovation," which is perhaps an explanation for some forms of deviance (the middle class may fit better in this regard), does not have much validity among disadvantaged youth.

In recapitulating our own findings, a number of fundamental issues are worth further delineation. As organized in the following table, several aspirational-expectational types materialize.

1. *High Aspiration-High Expectation-Realistic.* Of the high-aspirational group, this represents the largest proportion of youth studied. Many of the youth who aspire high have set about attempting to achieve their goals. They are fairly knowledgeable about the legitimate means by which these goals can be attained, and are aware of the obstacles which they are likely to encounter. *Paradoxically, most of this group represents distinguishably non-delinquent youth* with many of its members actively engaged in the achievement process. They characteristically regard deviant and delinquent behavior as inappropriate to their objectives and therefore as maladaptive. One might say that these youth have some predictable expectation to succeed. They, as much as anyone, truly represent the Horatio Alger myth.

2. *High Aspiration-High Expectation-Unrealistic.* These youth are a small proportion of the high aspirational group. They engage in considerable fantasy about achievement but at this point lack substantive knowledge about their objectives and the means to

Table 3. An Empirical Taxonomy of Aspirations and Expectations among Lower-Class Youth

High Aspirations (Empirically few — less than 25%)			
High Expectations		*Low Expectations*	
Realistic	*Unrealistic*	*Realistic*	*Unrealistic*
+ (many)	– (few)	+ (many)	– (very few)

Low Aspirations (Empirically high — more than 75%)			
Equivalent Expectations	*Low Expectations*	*Atonic*	*Exploratory*
Realistic	*Realistic–Unrealistic*	*Unrealistic*	*Realistic*
+ (most)	– (very few)	– (few)	– (few)

attain them. We would predict that hard reality ultimately will intervene and they will lower their expectations (and aspirations) at a future time.

In order to avoid repetition when describing all the remaining categories, it should be stated that the rate of delinquency appearing in this group is *no greater than any of the others, and is roughly equivalent in each of them.* Put another way, the following six categories exhibit similar rates of delinquency, and disjunctures between aspirations and expectations, wherever they may exist, are not significantly related to delinquency among the lower class youth studied. It should again be emphasized that *nondelinquency* (or a low rate of it) appears only in Type 1.

3. *High Aspiration–Low Expectation–Realistic.* Among the high-aspiration group, these represent the second largest category. These are youth who realize the problems of achieving success and have come down with a severe jolt from their lofty ambitions.

Some delinquency appears *but not disproportionately* when compared to other types. This would in all probability be the group in which, according to Merton, and Cloward and Ohlin, a large proportion of delinquency would appear. Yet we find them generally adaptive and willing to settle for less than what they once would.

4. *High Aspiration–Low Expectation–Unrealistic.* This category is extremely rare. It would include youth who had considerable ambition and for some reason lowered their expectations; yet they are those who with some effort might very well be able to achieve high goals.

5. *Low Aspiration–Equivalent Expectation–Realistic.* This type represents the largest proportion by far of those youth interviewed. They are responsive to their own cultural environment and select occupations (income, residence) which are found most often among adults in the community and set their sights on achieving similar socioeconomic status. Horatio Alger is essentially irrelevant to them and is not a "meaningful" value in the context of their community and social life. They are aspirationally adaptive and see no great difficulty in accomplishing their aims.

6. *Low Aspiration–Low Expectation–Unrealistic.* This group is empirically quite rare. Only occasionally do we find youth who aspire to occupations commonly found in their cultural setting and expect even lower results.

7. *Low Aspiration–Atonic–Unrealistic.* Occasionally during our interviewing we encountered youth who were extraordinarily listless and had no interest or hope in occupational placement. This group may ultimately gain some measure of interest in the occupational world, or they may begin to engage in "retreatist" activities such as drug addiction.

8. *Low Aspiration–Exploratory–Realistic.* These are highly individualistic youth who wish to move out and try many occupations, although their sights are now set on a fairly low level. They represent a small proportion of the total number interviewed. These youth, in possibly breaking away from the specific cultural milieu in which they have been reared, ultimately may develop higher aspirations through new culture contacts and subsequently higher socioeconomic status. At this juncture, however, they remain at a

relatively low level of hope and are representative of a generally existential mode. They may be those lower-class youth who occasionally crop up in "hippie" communities.

In the final analysis, even though our approach is highly qualitative, we offer the proposition that youth deviance is not a consequence of "illegitimate" innovation. Social scientists, perhaps with a view from the top, have assumed that middle class values impinge significantly upon lower class segments of society. We find little evidence to support that contention. As we shall point out in Chapter 9, delinquency can be explained by the concept of anomie, but a form of anomie different from that which has become sociologically commonplace. In some measure, this study has been designed to balance the scales of sociological empiricism. Culture, perhaps more significantly subculture, equalizes man's wishes and desires to a degree not altogether understood in the social sciences.

The logic of the Mertonian thesis, perhaps more than anything else, has fostered the belief that economic illusion has been more trenchant than bedrock economic reality. In this sense, man's illusions seem firmly anchored in the reality of his specific community, a reality both economic and moral — a condition only infrequently overridden even in "mass-media-ized" society. If our data are correct, we suggest that economic reality is more the case and, therefore, delinquency must be attributed to other determinants. In our view, the reality of moral disjuncture more than economoral disjuncture is at the root of youth deviance. We call this condition, "moral anomie," and suggest that it is not class-based or subcultural but that it pervades the entire society. In the chapter that follows, we explore this concept and its implications, again referring to youth and their conceptions (the result of cultural *and* subcultural socialization) of good and bad, right and wrong — notions we suggest are intrinsic to moral anomie.

Good Boy-Bad Boy 9

However anomic or alienated a person may be, he is never totally lacking in a sense of good and evil. That sense may outlast all capacity to communicate with other human beings; it can animate a psychotic (and in catatonic schizophrenia it can throttle, silence, and paralyze him) despite his narcissistic isolation from everyone else. Indeed, conceptions of right and wrong, of good and evil, are everpresent in any population of human beings regardless of how fully or superficially they have been socialized. Consequently, it is not surprising that we should have found these terms, applied by and to boys and girls, so meaningful and so productive for our purposes.

A Chicago boy says, "A good person don't do nothin'. A bad person does anything," vivid definitions so polarized that, armed with them, he is able to be contemptuous of the former while dissociating himself from the latter. We would expect respondents of any type to deny their wickedness (and they do so less than we would expect). We would also expect them to affirm their virtue (but if so, here again we are being too simple-minded). One finds rationalizations before the fact ("techniques of neutralization" as David Matza and Gresham Sykes have dubbed them)[1] and rationalizations after the fact used to justify

[1] David Matza and Gresham M. Sykes, "Juvenile Delinquency and Subterranean Values," *American Sociological Review, XXVI* (October, 1961), pp. 712–719.

disapproved conduct. They are often the same rationalizations that Matza and Sykes find among juvenile delinquents. We find them just as often among nondelinquents. No one, not even in the community of saints Emile Durkheim once asked his readers to envisage, where venial sins become deadly sins, can always bring value and action into perfect harmony. Furthermore, one man's value is another man's poison — neither has much to do with law-abiding or law-breaking behavior. All young people within society are somehow responsive to its controls; only the presocialized and the asocialized, for example, small children, mongoloid idiots, and psychotics, are somewhat less so. In gross terms, we may say that juvenile delinquents like juvenile nondelinquents are socialized, one no more or less than the other. To say this is not to deny that delinquents break rules which nondelinquents obey. But why they do certain things or abstain from doing them does not seem to us to be normatively determined.

The pioneer work of Mead, Cooley, Freud, Durkheim, and Piaget[2] has conditioned students of the subject to assume that socialization and normative determination are identical. Yet it is possible to be both socialized and anomic, to be conformist and normless. That this condition obtains in the large middle reaches of American society most of us have taken for granted, at least since David Riesman wrote *The Lonely Crowd*.[3] By middle-class other-direction, Riesman can only have meant a specific state of socialized deregulation such that Americans, as they responded less and less to inner promptings, came, through imitation, to look and act more and more alike. Widespread conformity may issue from circumstances that foster *socialization into anomie*, with people seeking surface cues to replace the norms they no longer internalize. Such conformity, with standard deviation, is observ-

---

[2]George Herbert Mead, *Mind, Self and Society* (Chicago: University of Chicago Press, 1934); Charles Horton Cooley, *Social Organization: A Study of the Larger Mind* (New York: C. Scribner, 1916); Sigmund Freud, *A General Introduction to Psychoanalysis* (New York: Liveright Publishing Co., 1935); Emile Durkheim, *Rules of Sociological Method* (Chicago: University of Chicago Press, 1938); Jean Piaget, *The Moral Judgment of Children* (London: K. Paul, Trench, Trubner and Co., Ltd., 1932).

[3]David Riesman, *The Lonely Crowd* (New Haven: Yale University Press, 1950).

ably present in the American middle class. No one should be astounded that it is also observably present in the American underclass.

Of late, and with good reason, much has been made of the identity crisis facing middle-class Americans. Large numbers of them have been plagued by the question of who they are and what they are. Is there any reason for sociologists to doubt a priori that this anxiety is society-wide? Why should one suppose that lower-class persons have been unaffected by the general dislocation and wholesale deracination of our times? On the contrary, if many a middle- and upper-class person cannot locate his "true self" nor any active superego in his multiple self, then how much more likely are people at a lower level to be afflicted in the same way. Such piecemeal evidence as we have indicates that they are. If so, then conscience, that heavy burden of prescriptions and prohibitions, is dead or dying from top to bottom in a society that has lost its bearings. Scratch the system anywhere (as Riesman and more recently, Kenneth Keniston did with college students,[4] as we do with youth in the slums), and unless we are much mistaken, you will find something like social psychopathy. Given their superior education, members of the middle class can verbalize the problem with greater skill than those who have had to attend slum schools. Given their superior income, they can seek professional help and psychiatric solace. A psychoanalyst like Allen Wheelis, judging by the vague malaise and diffuse contents of his own affluent patients, is able to offer a superb portrait of their trouble (and his) in a book appropriately entitled *The Quest for Identity*.[5] Following classical Freudian procedure, he peels off one layer of consciousness after another, only to encounter a great void. It is the same void we have encountered over and over among our economically-impoverished subjects.

The externals, the trappings, the phenotypic representations are as various as the colors on a spectrum; and the genotype, moral anomie itself, transcends them all. Sexual, chronological, socio-economic, ethnic, racial, and regional differences persist. We must

---

[4] Kenneth Keniston, *The Uncommitted* (New York: Basic Books, 1965).

[5] Allen Wheelis, *The Quest for Identity* (New York: Norton, 1958).

reckon with them in attempting to make any sensible analysis or useful prediction: and to do so is to negate the culture of poverty as a viable concept. Microsociologically, it breaks down into too many important variables, but by the same token, macrosociologically, poverty as such loses all significance. Nearly thirty years ago, Edwin Sutherland dispelled the notion that poverty, or traits associated with poverty, caused crime.[6] He acknowledged that poor and disreputable people commit crimes — while drawing attention to the fact that rich and reputable people also commit crimes. Offenders in the upperworld and in the underworld, he pointed out, were internally differentiated into groups of abortionists, fee splitters, pickpockets, confidence men, and so forth. At the same time Sutherland contended, they were all subject to two major forces which he designated as: differential association and social disorganization. Sutherland's insights have yet to be exhausted even in criminology proper. It is nevertheless possible and desirable to carry them farther afield. If we retain differential association as more or less equivalent to socialization, and alter the amorphous "social disorganization" into anomie, much can be learned about American society and all of its subgroups. With this conceptual scheme, we need not slight real and vital differences; Sutherland knew that embezzlement and misrepresentation had to be distinguished from bootlegging and safe-cracking; criminality and delinquency, like life style in general, is obviously class-typed. To study the unlawful acts of corporation executives is one thing; to study racketeering in the organized underworld is another. Still, a judicious application of the scheme makes it possible to trace a red thread of common processes through the whole system.

Independently-written reports on our three groups of poverty-stricken, ethnically diversified youth, highlight that red thread — the moreso for self-evaluation (good boy–bad boy, good girl–bad girl) since its presence is not nearly so marked in any other area of the inquiry. Here perhaps we come to the heart of the matter: there is a certain sameness of responses that rules out "blind" attribution of origin. Those who hold to the "culture of poverty"

[6]Edwin H. Sutherland, *White Collar Crime* (New York: Dryden Press, 1949).

theory might claim further support for their position in these findings. On the other hand, following Sutherland, we suspect that our data point to something more like a universal phenomenon. To proceed additively by piling one variable on top of another, using poverty as a base, has so far proved to be sterile in criminological research. Practically everybody violates the criminal law; some poor people do not; many rich people do. Selective sanctions are another matter. Poverty substantially accounts for *punishment*, but it is no more criminogenic than wealth. Crime, as an American way of life, is deeply and systemically embedded in the social fabric. Why that should be so is, ultimately, something we need to know. For the present, it behooves serious investigators to move modestly in a broader Copernican direction, and to separate common from discrete conditions while striving to attain a more appropriate general theory.

Images of the Self

We have discovered that the terms, good boy and bad boy (as well as good girl and bad girl), no matter what connotations they may have for the public at large, are loaded with meaning for young people. They — and as it turned out, their older siblings and their parents — responded without hesitation to questions we raised about the content and the significance of these words. Their answers provide considerable insight into the adolescent's self-image and his image of others — plus further light on prevailing systems of morality.

At one extreme, we behold the oversocialized boy or girl who is utterly incapable of making his own independent judgments of good and bad. He unquestioningly accepts the visible and official, the certified and respectable judgments of society. He does this even when negative judgments are passed on *him*, and even when he considers himself innocent of accusations on which those judgments are based.[7] Consider the case of a New York boy who has been

[7]For a general discussion of "deviance by definition," see Edwin M. Lemert, *Social Pathology* (New York: McGraw-Hill, 1951); Howard S. Becker, *The Outsiders* (New York: Free Press of Glencoe, 1963).

consigned to a school for "the emotionally disturbed," and who for that reason alone, declares himself to be bad:

> [Do you think you are a bad boy?]
> Yeah.
> [Why?]
> Because I'm going to a 600 school.
> [And that makes you a bad boy?]
> I wouldn't be going there if I wasn't a bad boy.
> [Well, why did they send you there?]
> They said I was smoking cigarettes. They said I was trying to choke other boys. They said I was throwing firecrackers out the bathroom window. They said I was hitting the teacher.
> [And were you doing all those things?]
> I didn't throw firecrackers out the window. I didn't try to choke no guy. I didn't smoke no cigarette. I did hit the teacher — after she scratched me in the face . . . and twisted my arm around. I tried to break away, and then I went like that, and I hit her in the lip.

Knowledge of his own conduct, in this case, of his own innocence, is eclipsed by an authoritative judgment to the contrary. He reasons: since I have been relegated to a school for bad boys, I *am* a bad boy. The frequency with which boys and girls manifest such logic has been duly noted most recently by John M. Martin and Joseph P. Fitzpatrick in their excellent handbook, *Delinquent Behavior:* " . . . When we, by gossip or rumor, label a particular child a "bad boy"; when we, as a term of disapprobation, call (by word or deed) a young man a "hoodlum," we may very well be contributing to establishing him as such, both in his own mind (because what he thinks he is depends heavily upon what others say he is), and in the minds of others such as parents, friends, peers, local shopkeepers, policemen, and school teachers who treat him according to some status and role. Once the status-role of bad boy, delinquent or hoodlum has been assigned, and perhaps reinforced by an arrest or two, and possibly even a trip to juvenile court and '12 and 6' (18 months) at the local training school or reformatory, then the Dramatization of Evil ('tagging, defining, identifying, segregating, describing, emphasizing, making conscious and self-conscious') is nearly complete. Our young man *is* a hood: others think he is a hood; he thinks he is a hood; others exclude him from many legitimate roles in school, work, friendships, and even the armed forces. At best he is permitted only menial or illegitimate roles; if his offense is reprehensible enough, nothing is left open to him — he is a pariah, literally an outlaw."[8]

Conversely, a favorable self-image may be preserved regardless of actual misbehavior, so long as heteronomous youth is able to avoid a head-on collision with official society. The oversocialized boy, once branded as bad, so brands himself:

> [Are you a good boy or a bad boy?]
> Now that I'm in trouble, I'm a bad boy.
> [But you say you didn't steal anything.]
> Yeah, but I'm still in trouble.

The rule of moral expediency, by which our youth are governed, is not differentiated by sex. For this reason, a New York girl who thinks sexual promiscuity is wrong, makes her objection to it on purely pragmatic grounds. She feels that "scheming around" with boys produces too great a loss of face. Once your sexual availability is well known, "Around our neighborhood, they just put you aside," you are disesteemed and your marriageability is reduced. Getting pregnant is a real problem, but it becomes catastrophic if you do not know which of several boys has caused your plight. Therefore, be virtuous.

An adolescent unwed mother flatly asserts that, "There is no good girls really," and then, a little later, softens her indictment, for she means, "There isn't any good, *good* girls." Finally she clarifies her view (much as we would and as well as we could): "I mean, you find girls who are obedient, but you will not find girls who are good."

Although in the framework of goodness, girls stress appearance, manners, clothes, cleanliness more than boys do, they are also more wary about mere facade — which is a snare and a delusion:

---

[8]John M. Martin and Joseph P. Fitzpatrick, *Delinquent Behavior: A Redefinition of the Problem* (New York: Random House, 1966), 81–82.

> There's girls that they go to school regularly, and they stay clean. They keep out of trouble. They never have to go to court. That's what we consider a good girl. But, usually those good girls are the ones that have the devil in them. They're the ones that turn out to be no good.

The same idea expressed by another girl:

> The good girls are supposed to be the quiet ones. We say, the quiet ones are the sneaky ones. They're always sneaking on their mother and everything. But a bad girl tells her mother what she does. She don't hide it. Like some girls are quiet, and they say, "Oh, I don't do this. I don't drink or anything," but . . . they do it all. You know, and they're supposed to be so good and high and mighty.

An occasional youngster (more often female than male) will seek absolution by shifting blame onto others who have corrupted him or her. Evil consists less in doing bad than in teaching it, or taunting and coercing others into it:

> Like robbing. Someone tells you, "We're going to rob a place," and you listen, not knowing what he knows, that you're going to end up in jail or in a home, telling you, "Oh, you're a punk or a fool," or something like that, you know, if you don't do it . . . And the only one that's bad is the one teaching the other one. He knows he's doing wrong, but he thinks he's going to get someplace by getting the other guy to go along.

Thus do the Children of Darkness corrupt the Children of Light. Theirs is an unpardonable offense, for they prey upon the innocent:

> Rita got me to go to this hardware, you know, and I thought me and her were good friends. But, anyhow, she said she'd beat me up if I didn't go to the hardware and steal this glue. She said she'd beat my head in. So, I mean I was scared of her at the time. I did what she told me to. And my mother never found out until she went and told my mother, and I said, "Mother what am I supposed to do?"

Mother told her. "Golly, She. . . . You should of seen what she done to me. I thought she was going to beat me to death." In short, a girl shoplifts in order to escape physical assault; the act is revealed to a stern mother — and results in physical assault. In this game of heads I win, tails you lose, the offender is able to picture herself as a victim — not of such grand abstractions as "society," but of those in her immediate surroundings.

Wrongdoing may be avoided even under intense peer-group pressure, but only, or most effectively, if one is heavily fortified by fright, which is a substitute for — or gets to be equated with — conscience. In Chicago, a girl who never goes shoplifting herself, admits that she once went along with a friend. "She done it, but I didn't . . . And she got caught. . . . They called her parents, who weren't home, and then they called the cops. The cops came and got her, but they made me go home. They said I didn't do anything." Why didn't she do anything? "Because I was scared. I just knew I'd get caught." Finally, as an afterthought: "I would have had a guilty conscience, you know."

For most of our adolescents, very little is intrinsically wrong. From this point of view, immorality consists not so much in certain acts, but in the *discovery* of those acts. Evil stems more from detection than from commission. Nothing has happened until it is known to have happened by those who are authorized to make one's private actions into public scandals. This attitude is precisely the one Branislaw Malinowski delineated years ago in describing Trobriand Islanders,[9] whose youth went unpunished for the violation of sacred sexual tabus — unless they were given publicity, which insured remorseless punishment. Early in his fieldwork, Malinowski witnessed the suicide of a young Trobriand boy who had been denounced by a rival for having breached the incest tabu. The boy felt no great guilt and suffered no special shame for criminal conduct known to many; its exposure and public condemnation, required him to climb a tall tree and plung to his death. Malinowski, as he dug deeper and deeper into Trobriand society, learned that this case was paradigmatic. His nonliterate people, young and old alike, were no more slavishly bound to law, with all its super-

[9]Branislaw Malinowski, *Crime and Custom in Savage Society* (London: K. Paul, Trench, Trubner and Co., Ltd., 1926).

natural sanctions, than modern man. Either could "do" anything, neither could survive the inexorability of justice after certain unforseeable forces actuated people to make an issue of everyday transgressions.

Malinowski's analysis fits our data much better than the work of most professional criminologists. It also makes our respondents look statistically normal. In all probability, most people, while undersocialized in the sense that they do not have well-developed superegos, are oversocialized in the sense that their self-image is distinguished from their social image. If, consciously or unconsciously committed to this oversocialized conception of ethics, they are nothing but what society says they are. When they see themselves exactly as others see them, there is no self except "the looking-glass" self.

Crime statistics are notoriously misleading because they grossly distort the nature and the incidence of unlawful deviation in any American community. In addition, crime statistics fail to reflect the social pathology of any particular individual. Nevertheless, it is obvious that whether or not a teenager is branded as a delinquent, will be of the utmost importance to him. For self-perception and the perception of others, this circumstance may well be decisive.

There are those in our sample who, although they have committed only very petty offenses, and these but rarely, characterize themselves as "bad" solely because they were apprehended. Being "caught" means that henceforth they are assigned, and they accept, their status as delinquents. Invert the situation and it still holds: career delinquents whose behavior patterns are consistently unlawful (through their possible involvement in the drug traffic or the numbers racket), who have escaped arrest (sometimes by chance, often as a result of protection) — overwhelmingly define themselves as "pretty good," "just like everybody else," and "not so bad," and the like. Appearances are widely understood to be deceptive, but they eventually merge with reality, the truth will out, and that truth is external to the individual. In the long run, there is no difference between the social self and the private self. That this conviction should prevail at a developmental stage in which young people are struggling to attain the definitive boundaries of their identity is no small issue.

A View of the World

The adolescent tends not only to draw his self-image from the salient institutional world that encapsulates him, he simultaneously perceives the pecking order of that world in much the same terms. Self-definition, which originates outside his own consciousness, is projected back onto the external world of significant and insignificant others. A formula emerges. Slightly simplified it reads, "What *I* am, others are too."

For example, a young Washington girl who has had many illicit sexual relationships and regards herself as both good and bad, when asked what a good girl is, says, "I don't think there are any good girls." The interview proceeds:

> [You don't think there are any?]
> I don't know of any. All the girls I thought were good and pure and never had anything to do with boys, I found out they weren't doing anything but fooling the public.
> [Just like everybody else?]
> Yeah. They just kept everything secret. But sooner or later people find out.

Again, from the same group, a self-confessed but so far unlabeled pathological deviant who asserts, like many of his peers, that he is both good and bad, states:

> I've done a whole lot of things that was wrong. I have raped people. I have did everything.
> Even bad children got some good in them . . . I've got a little bit of good. I mean I got good.
> What's good? I'm living and I eat. I mean, I do things for people. Like if somebody says, "Look, I need food. I'm hungry," I give 'em money. I say, "Here."

Then, to round out his ruminations:

> Everybody is doing something wrong.

When placed in the dominant moral calculus, this thought may be translated as, "Everybody runs the risk of getting caught." And, since he has avoided arrest, he is innocent, an evaluation in which he believes that his mother concurs.

Once its explicitness has been established time and again, all ambiguity about the moral criterion disappears, and it is as freely applied to others as to oneself. Here are illustrative excerpts that deserve to be quoted at some length. From New York:

[Would you say that you're a good boy?]
Yeah.
[Nothing bad about you?]
No.
[Then these things like hitting a teacher and carrying a gun are not bad?]
No.
[Smoking pot is not bad?]
No.
[What would you say a bad boy is?]
Always getting into trouble, always getting sent up.
[If you don't get caught, then you are not a bad boy?]
No.
[You're only bad if you get caught?]
Yeah.
[Why does that make you bad? You don't have much luck?]
Mostly luck.
[Then the difference between a good boy and a bad boy is luck?]
Yeah.
[Do you really believe that?]
Yeah.
[You mean if you killed someone and got away with it, you wouldn't be bad?]
You're good, sure.
[Well, what's the worst thing that anybody can do?]
What do you mean?
[To anybody else.]
Mostly beat them up.
[Not kill them?]
No.
[Why is it worse to beat them up than to kill them?]
Because, it hurts, man, it pains,

Some of this may be synthetic, merely put on to deceive the interviewer. That it nonetheless has some substance we learn from the startling responses to another question along the same lines, namely, "Which is worse: smoking pot or mugging?" put to teenagers in New York who by and large insist that marijuana is harmless. A majority claim that smoking pot is worse than mugging. The reason is simple: if you are caught smoking pot, even though you injure no one, the sentence is stiffer than if you are caught mugging and inflicting an injury on someone else.

For our population, badness isn't all that bad, and goodness isn't all that good. Thus this exchange in Chicago:

> [How do you feel about some of the things that you've been doing, like burglary, breaking in on people's homes? Does that bother you at all?]
> It don't bother me that much, when I'm broke. If I had money I wouldn't ever do it.
> [While you were working, did you ever do anything like that?]
> Naw. When I was working I stayed drunk all the time.
> [Why would you stay drunk all the time?]
> Something to do. Go to the show Friday, play poker Saturday. Then get drunk. Not every week, I didn't do that.
> [Do you ever think that some of the things the guys do, like robbing and burglarizing, is bad?]
> I used to tell 'em about that — when I never done it before . . . I said, "Now, what's you go and do that for?" They didn't think nothin' of it — I did that until I started going. I never did go in; I just stayed outside. I don't think that's so bad but still it's the same thing as going in.
> [Would you say that anybody who does that is bad then?]
> Not really that bad.

If a violation of the law seldom induces guilt, it sometimes produces exultation. A boy who believes that, "No one's good, and a lot of people [like himself] are bad," likes to "hit" cabs, skirting danger, courting trouble, "feeling good inside" when he has had a close shave: "Watching a guy get mad and letting him chase you. That's what I like." The experience is just "scary" enough to make it thrilling; burglary, which "can get you into more trouble," is less appealing for that reason. But moderately risky lawbreaking yields legitimate kicks. There is the pure pleasure of outrunning and outwitting a respectable antagonist, of robbing kids who have better clothes, of boasting that: "We *all* bad."

For something about goodness is suspect. Good guys are. "Them cats with their hair real short. They wear white gym shoes and look pretty good all day. They're frail, in other words . . . Everybody got their own styles, I guess. Frails like to be frails, and we like to be like we are." Lengthy concrete, referential lists of bad behavior, overlapping legal classifications, are easy to elicit. A bad boy steals, cusses, drinks, rapes, fights, sniffs glue, takes drugs. He talks back to his mother, stays out late at night. A bad girl "puts out" for anyone and everyone. Getting caught and being punished for such acts makes youth bad. What then is goodness? The question baffles many respondents, causing some who are otherwise voluble to be tongue-tied. To be good is to be nice, to obey, to have manners. But "good" is most often defined negatively as the opposite of "bad." It is an abstract category with little behavioral content, an "act" of omission. Not being bad is being good. Not to steal, not to fight, not to look for trouble is to be good. After having dilated at length on bad behavior, one Washington youth, generally articulate and sensitive to questioning, is stymied.

> [What's your definition of a good boy?]
> Well, let's just say it's the opposite of that [a bad boy].
> [How about girls? How would you define a good girl?]
> [Laugh] That's very hard for me to put into words. I mean I couldn't really answer that — so I might as well not talk, 'cause I'm liable to get tumbled up with words. I couldn't answer that. Not right now. I mean it would really take some thought. I possibly could if I tried, but right off the bat, I couldn't say.

To a New York boy, the good kid is one who, "Don't do nothing. He be good. He don't carry nothing on him." We wonder if he ever met a kid like that: "No." Are there any really good kids on the street? "Yeah. They little kids, two, three years old. They can't do nothing. Carry a knife, maybe they could pick it up, but they couldn't put it in their pocket." Not to be bad is to be good — and to be good is hardly to be anything at all. Good boys and girls are formless, featureless, passive receptors; they "keep to themselves"; they are "quiet"; they "stay alone"; they "don't hang around with other kids" — which makes them apparitions, ciphers, shadows, isolates hovering outside the mainstream of youthful activity. Those who are "bad" act bad; those who are "good" do not act; they scarcely exist. Inaction leads to inanition as goodness is purified and etherealized into nothingness.

While the good is impalpable and unreal, the bad can be seen everywhere. And to have been very bad, to have been through the crucible, has its advantages. A young lady who is still in her teens, but raising an illegitimate child asserts that, "I'm not too good now, but I'm an angel compared to what I used to be. I smoke reefers once in a blue moon. Before it was every day . . . I come out into the street and I hang around with my friends and we drink and we have times together. But it's not like it was when I went out with a crowd of girls looking for fights." All "the stupid things" she used to do helped her to grow up fast, taught her about life, made it possible for her to improve later on, to stay human, to be realistic after she "grew up and matured a little bit mentally." Nor does she regard her experience as unusual:

> Oh, no, there's a lot of girls like that. Take my cousin. She was one of the biggest hoodlums on this street, and now if you see her . . . She's so sophisticated that you'd never think that she was the President of the Sweethearts [Gang]. She looks very decent compared to what she used to be when she was a teenager.

Another girl describes her friends as "half-and-half." As for herself, "I can't say I'm good and I can't say I'm bad because I got good and bad in me." We pursue the matter:

> [Would you say you're better than you used to be?]
> Yes.
> [Were you good or bad before?]
> I was terrific.
> [Terrific?]
> I was bad, very bad.

The equation of "very bad" and "terrific" slips out, interlarded with a little laughter, and then, more seriously: "Well, I don't go stealing all the time any more. And I'm more matured than I used to be. I mean, you know, I act ladylike. I used to act like a hoodlum, a girl that just stayed in the street any time. Not now . . . As the years go by you get more matured."

Unknown or unpunished deviation is widely viewed, then, as a stage one passes through and outgrows all the more swiftly for having experienced it in the first place. Objectively, we have good reason to know something most of our informants tell us, that, "There's no difference whatsoever," in the acts of boys and girls who get stigmatized as delinquents and those who do not. Or as one New York girl puts it: "There's some that do things worse than those that get police records, and there's kids that don't have police records at all that do some of the funniest things." Another girl whose boyfriend had been sent away to a training school, deplores his desire for notoriety:

> He's always looking for bad stuff. He tries to be known. When you try to be known, you have a record. You go to jail. That makes you a *big* boy. You have a rep and you say, "Oh, I been to jail."

In a large part of this milieu, recognition comes with "bigness," "knowness" and "badness." And "goodness" exacts a toll perhaps as high as "badness."

The Moral Code

The polarization of these concepts, put into reciprocal action terms, does not appear to be simply a semantic device. Almost every decision to classify specific acts under one or another of the mutually exclusive categories emanates from standards located in semisacred American institutions: the school (whence comes self-assessment of intelligence and achievement potential), the law, and the family. Reference to God or Church or revered spiritual leaders as sources of moral judgment are noticeably scarce. In no instance do our respondents allude even remotely to theological or broadly ideological considerations. Deviation and conformity are perceived in strictly concrete behavioral forms — underscoring the morally anomic condition operative in this population.[10] Self-evaluation goes like this:

> I know I'm not the . . . you know, most honest person in the world. But I ain't really dishonest. I mean I'm a little dishonest . . . I don't suppose I'm that dishonest. I never steal from my friends, and I never steal from my brother.
> [What kinds of faults do you have?]
> Burglarizing homes, that's a fault . . . no good. I don't know. Stay out late. That's a bad thing. My aunt, she'll ask me to be in by 11:00 p.m. Sometimes I do, sometimes I don't come in till 1, 2, that's bad.

Another youth:

> I'm pretty good, I guess.
> [How about your stealing?]
> I just call it borrowing, ambushing. I just borrowed it for the time being. I'm a good burglar, I'm smart, I ain't got caught yet.
> [What are your bad points?]
> Fightin', cards — losing. Unlucky at cards and girls.

A "good Chicago boy" tells us:

> I don't sniff glue or take dope or nothin' like that. I don't go around robbin' and doin' stuff like that on purpose. At least, not all the time. Don't hang around in gangs . . .
> [What is a good boy?]
> Does everything his mother and father asks, he respects 'em, respects the teachers, respects who he works with.

A 17-year-old boy says:

> I'm in between. No one's good and lot of people are bad, I'm closer to being bad. I'm stupid.
> [Probe as to nature of peer group.]

---

[10] It is the same condition, with the same nonideological focus, similarly oriented to the present, which Kenneth Keniston reports for his "alienated" and "overprivileged" Harvard students. See *The Uncommitted* (New York: Basic Books, 1965).

We all bad, we don't do things on the side of the law. Good boys stay inside the law.

An experienced burglar and leader says:

. . . good and bad I guess . . . bad when I'm taking things. Good when I'm stayin' away from people's stuff . . . just average. [What is a good boy?]
. . . probably call 'em a giant boob . . . but he's a lot smarter boob, 'cause at least he knows he's never gonna get in trouble.

As we have already suggested, institutional sources for standards are more often explicitly cited by girls, to explain their conformity, than by boys. The girls mention personal attributes, such as clean clothes, neat and conservative dress, nice speech, friendliness, warmth, and empathy, as distinctive criteria used to assess their worth as well as that of others, to a greater degree than the boys.

You don't run around with the bad kind of people, and always listen to your elders, which can explain everything to you if you listen just right. I'm really in between . . . no angel, but I go to school every day, and I don't hang around with boys by myself, don't run out in the middle of the street and stuff like that. Sometimes I don't listen to Mom, I'll fuss back at my sister when she starts fussin'. [Respondent never steals] because I just didn't wanta lose my reputation . . . I'm the only one of my whole family that's never ditched school or anything.

What's the difference between a good and a bad girl?

The way she talks . . . around the boys. Some of these girls that are in school, they don't care what they say, some of 'em take . . . dope. A lot of the kids around school, you can just tell, by lookin' at 'em in their actions, sometimes, that they do. [Good] . . . someone that can talk to people and that's got a real nice personality and doesn't hang around with the wrong crowd or something like that. They're always saying something that's not nice to hear or something. And it's not only the girls, it's to the boys.
One that doesn't cuss and smoke and steal anything, stuff like that. Girls that goes around and steals every time you turn

> around and is cussing all the time, and takes things that doesn't belong. Flirt with boys.
>
> If they're dressed nice, have clean things and have clean body . . . She'd be all sloppy, wouldn't comb her hair, wear all sloppy dresses, wouldn't be clean and would be stealing, and hittin' others.

Only one female youth offered anything like a sociocultural explanation for girls that are bad:

> Some experience she had that influenced her . . . lead her to start drinking, smoking, swearing, sexual things not out of love but just out of sex.

These examples clearly indicate that our youth only exceptionally offer an explanation for their good or bad attributes. Moreover, there is an extreme lack of self-denigration. No one is in a repenting mood; there is no quest for a psychic solution which would resolve inner conflicts and feelings of ambivalence or assuage the imperceptible sense of guilt brought on by their confessions.

Our cluster of good–bad questions produces something like a bell-shaped curve. A few see themselves and their associates as all bad ("there's no such thing as a good kid"), and a few are oblivious to anything but "good kids" like themselves. But, overwhelmingly, their answers are mixed: "I'm somewhere in between," "I'm not exactly an angel," "Sometimes I'm good and sometimes I'm bad," "I'm not good and I'm not bad," "I'm half-and-half," "I consider myself bad and good," "I'm normal — some ways good, some ways bad," and so on and on. Moreover, the child who thinks he is such a mixture, thinks the same of everyone else. (However, that bell-shaped distribution of self-definition corresponds more to adjudicative definition, the social labeling, than the deviant behavioral patterns of action.)

There is an overarching attitude toward this mixed interpretation of human nature, namely, the unquestioning but abstract acceptance of parental codes. Adherence to those codes produces the good, their violation the bad in all of us. Guilt and shame, insofar as they exist, are the products of disobedience. Failure to heed *mother* is the source of all further transgressions. To an out-of-wedlock mother we interviewed, no girl is wholly good because none is completely honest. At least this is her spontaneous opinion; it means a good girl would "never have told even a little lie." She would never have stolen or fought or "schemed" but, above all, she would "always, always have been obedient." We want to know whether she is describing a girl or an angel, and she responds, "Well, that's what I'm trying to say — there is no good girl." It is easier for her to delineate the "real bad girl" as follows:

> She has no respect for anybody, always fighting, cursing — can't control her tongue, drinking, smoking, looking for trouble . . . She's always trying to throw herself at boys, trying to be very sexy, trying to show everything she's got, but she ain't got nothing . . . She has sex with different people and is proud of it, she broadcasts it . . .

The portrait is consistently harsh, and her self-portrait is only a little softer: "I have some good things and a lot of bad things in me." Whichever way the balance tips, a girl is undone finally by disregarding *mother*. She herself could have been redeemed at the penultimate moment by paying proper heed to maternal advice:

> When I was engaged to X, he used to come to my house and take me out. Once I took the ring off and threw it at him, because I got sick of hearing him say I was always playing with him. So my mother picked the ring up and she put it back on my finger. And then he said it again, and I took it off, and threw it at him. Then he started crying — so I told him "Why should you cry over a girl who is always playing with you?" And that's one thing I did wrong 'cause at the time I didn't know I was two months pregnant. I should have waited 'cause my mother had gave me permission when I was sixteen that we could get married. Me, the fool, I couldn't wait.

"Being nice with mother," "Doing like she says" — boys and girls repeatedly, ritualistically, repeat some such maxim. Although fathers or father substitutes are called upon to act as disciplinarians in the administration of corporal punishment, it is the mother who symbolizes morality. It is from her lips that the admonitions, which are later ruefully recollected, have fallen. Few can bring themselves to criticize mothers who are described elsewhere by the same respondents as having lived far from exemplary lives and who in many cases are represented by youngsters as having driven them to such hysteria and rage as to produce the very behavior which is forbidden. Only one male informant in his twenties has sufficient detachment to turn the tables, charging the mothers more than their progeny with irresponsibility:

> A lot of the mothers on our street are not married. They just want to live with a man. They have kids and don't really watch out for them. They let their kids play out in the street. There's no recreation area — and no one to come or give them, or even to look at them. No one gives them a start.

The same informant (a young man who thinks his salvation lay in being sent away from the street to Catholic schools even though the same exile had no such salutary effect on his numerous brothers and sisters) also adopts a heterodox position — but one that is much more baffling — on the subject of "taking things from little kids." This offense is widely regarded as more heinous than any other — so that boys who brag about stealing from other boys say they make it a point of honor not to steal from smaller ones. After awhile, in answer to our question. "What's the worst thing a boy can do?" we came to expect the frequent retort, "Take things from little kids." Whether this answer was truthful or not is another matter. It may only have been offered by way of consolation, to establish that the respondent was not utterly depraved. In any case, our more adult informant replies, "Well, I think that the worst thing he could do is, at the age of sixteen, have a child from a girl and quit school and not work and go on living with his parents . . ." A formidable bill of particulars, and not surprising, as this exchange is:

> [How about taking things from smaller kids?]
> Well, that's something no one can change. It's happening and it always will be happening.
> [But isn't that very bad?]

Well, it's one of the things I wouldn't consider bad. I call that one of the normal things in the world.

The logic here is even more involuted:

[Suppose a little kid has money and a big kid comes over and grabs it?]
Well, this is what makes these kids of today very slick and very clever. It's the first point of learning. When you own something, you must keep it to yourself. If I walked down the street showing everybody that I have five dollars, I wouldn't blame that person for taking it. If a young kid walks around tempting somebody, I think that somebody should take it away from him.

This is of a piece with his view that big kids should slap little kids who "decide they're getting wise" and keep them in line that way, an extension of the punitive technique already in force. The view is important because it comes from a truly rehabilitated "bad boy" who plans to devote himself to community service by keeping others from going astray. He is capable of real sensitivity:

Kids go to school in this neighborhood, and the teachers speak to them very cruelly. And the kid who comes from Puerto Rico, how you speak to him is how he learns to speak back. And a lot of them get emotionally disturbed. So they come home, and their parents may be about five feet four, and the kid happens to grow up a little bit taller or the same size. He goes to school — and the school teaches him different things than the parents who have no education. So the kid is outslicking his own parents.

These are shrewd observations and they have some diagnostic value. The bewilderment and insecurity of parents — and the decay of their authority in a foreign environment — are certainly symptomatic of deregulation or anomie. A generalized moral vacuum is created when parents lose confidence in old but no longer appropriate norms which they cannot successfully transmit any more than teachers are able to convey the values of modern urban middle-class society. Absorbing fragments of both, the child of either sex is ordinarily socialized to the point where he can experience conflict — while lacking psychic resources to resolve it. He is erratically but steadily punished and seldom rewarded. And yet, it is possible to emerge, to rise a bit above this bind, only to favor, as our reformed gang boy does, still more physical punishment. He would have the fathers "take out a belt and whack the kids" more than they now do.

We discover in all this a kind of *moral absolutism* or *moral realism*, the term used by Jean Piaget to indicate an early stage in child development, presumably replaced at a later stage by *moral relativism;* the awareness that rules are man-made and flexible.[11] For example, in the first stage a child fails to distinguish between acts committed with malice aforethought and those that are accidental. Therefore, he is inclined to judge himself more severely than he is judged by those who have attained a higher degree of maturity. Few residents of our study blocks seem to have moved much beyond moral absolutism, applied to themselves. Tired professionals, schoolteachers, caseworkers, clergymen — also apply it to them. The punitive law of Emile Durkheim is much more apparent in this world than the *cooperative* or *restitutive law* he took to be characteristic of modern civilization.[12] Exasperated adults, exasperated "do-gooders," and the children who seek to please or to defy them, are caught in the same net. Confusing neglect, dismay, and capricious punishment with permissiveness, they flay one and reinforce the other — its demonstrated ineffectiveness notwithstanding.

"Good and bad boy," as well as "good and bad girl," have personal meanings with objective correlatives we hope to work out more fully on further study and more analysis. For the largest proportion of youth, we believe that the adjectives will have to be hyphenated. Most of them, like most of the rest of us, are, as they contend, good-and-bad. It should be possible to construct a continuum embracing the whole juvenile population. We are sure that wherever specific individuals are ultimately placed on this con-

---

[11]Jean Piaget, *The Moral Judgment of Children* (London: K. Paul, Trench, Trubner and Co., Ltd., 1932).

[12]Emile Durkheim, *The Division of Labor in Society* (New York: Macmillan, 1933).

tinuum, there will be no significant correspondence between it and the official delinquent–nondelinquent records. If this is true, then as conscientious social scientists, we will have to set administrative records aside as irrelevant to our task, as a "will-o'-the-wisp" whose pursuit has led us down one blind alley after another. Henceforth, it will be necessary to study the slum child — good, bad, or indifferent — in all his complexity as a human being. To assume this burden is to relinquish a statistical artifact — and good riddance to it!

A Brief Recapitulation

Good riddance to statisticism notwithstanding, one aim of this work has been a modest attempt at rebalancing the empirical scale. This is no small task in criminological research, which is still so heavily dependent on "official statistics." In offering this detailed information, the result of qualitative techniques which in many sociological circles have achieved a second-class status to more "rigorous" quantitative methodology, our empiricism is necessarily selective and limited. Here we do not wish to argue the merits of one approach or the other; each assuredly has its contributions to make. All the same, it behooves us to reiterate the fundamental rationale with which we have proceeded.

As we (and others) have noted, the study of deviance, crime, and juvenile delinquency has placed considerable emphasis on the value of "official statistics" — that is, data collected by law enforcement and other administrative agencies whose function is that of social control. Despite innumerable protestations and apologias, the *reality* of delinquency — our capacity to describe even such basic elements as its location, frequency and type — has essentially escaped us. This we believe to be a major issue in delinquency research which is repeatedly confronted with the problem of getting the empirical horse to drink the theoretical water. We suggest that the qualitative approach is a useful and necessary strategy. It stems from the recognition of a vast and long-standing hiatus. The limitations of a radical empiricism rooted in statistical artifacts have substantially blocked more than they have facilitated our understanding of delinquency and its connections with the larger social process.

In this sense, the thrust of our inquiry has been directed toward examining two noteworthy theoretical contributions which have gained great favor within the past few years. The concept of the "culture of poverty," though not designed as an explanation of delinquency, has had a profound impact in the criminological world. That people of poverty are alike in sharing common economic circumstances is obvious and indisputable. That they similarly interpret and respond to their common condition is much less certain. This principle is surely applicable to youth as well as adults. If our observations are at all accurate, cross-cultural variations among the poor are marked — and not only in delinquency patterns but in many other social activities as well. From a sociological point of view, failure to recognize the validity of this proposition results in treating all low-income people as if they were a single social unit, which in turn produces frustration and despair. Social rehabilitationists know only two well what all this means when they engender counterproductive responses to their monolithic treatment, ideology, and program.

With respect to the other influential theory that fell within our purview, we have sought to explore the relationship between opportunity, aspirations, and delinquency. In the initial phase of our study, we began to be impressed by the general observation that most youth living in poverty were uninterested in high levels of educational or occupational achievement. In developing this material in depth, we observed that aspirations and commitment to the ideology of success were fraught with complexities. Although the preponderance of those in our study population ranked relatively low in aspiration (perhaps as a token of their immersion in the culture of poverty), the link between high aspiration and delinquency could not be established. More often, the reverse relationship obtained. The expectation that panacean programs of opportunity, though morally sound and otherwise worthy, will reduce delinquency seems to us to be unwarranted. This is emphatically not to say that such admirable programs should be abandoned. On the contrary, they are probably indispensible — but for other purposes.

Finally, we offer the general theory of moral anomie, pieced together largely from youthful conceptions of right and wrong, good and bad. Our conception is global, for we offer the basic proposition that anomie is not limited to those of lower socio-economic categories. It is society-wide, deriving not from economic privation but from the moral currents of contemporary social development. Modern urban-industrial life, having fragmented our social allegiances, loyalties, and commitments, also has shattered our capacity to live by the tenets of cooperative morality. The consequent deregulation and demoralization have little to do with class and much to do with modernity.[1] As rapid institutional change continues, and no matter how materially advantageous it may be, reliance on punitive law and the limits of restitutive law becomes more apparent. It is in this sense that delinquency and deviance in general are *declassed* and removed from the narrow economic interpretation that tends to dominate latterday sociological theory. Thus the relevance of *middle-class* delinquency and *white-collar* crime. Having noted — and then slighted — Sutherland's by now traditional effort to bridge this gap, sociologists also have avoided certain critical implications of his work. We have tried, in our small way, to refocus their attention, and — not incidentally — to help keep even more of us from becoming "Protean Men."

---

[1]Robert J. Lifton, "Protean Man," *Partisan Review* (Winter 1968), pp. 13–27. Reporting with keen insight on his psychiatric work in scattered parts of the world, Lifton has recently designated Modern Man as Protean Man — a nearly universal type devoid of anything like a stable superego or steady and operative conscience.

Eastern College Library
St. Davids, PA
3 1405 001 44409 4